In memory of Cesar, Roy, Gilorozco and each Marine who has laid down his life because of his commitment to protect American liberty.

"The very atmosphere of firearms anywhere and everywhere restrains evil interference—they deserve a place of honor with all that's good."

President George Washington

INTRODUCTION

Why listen to me? Like many of you, I've been shooting for most of my life. I joined the Marines at age 17 and did the first of what I consider "serious shooting" as a Reconnaissance Marine. Some of the DOD pistol training I received was good (such as the High-Risk Personnel course at Quantico). Some was not. Some of the guidance I was given was excellent. Some was not.

Later, as an officer, I had the privilege of serving as a founding member of the USMC Anti-Terrorism Battalion (ATBN). That period of my life provided the opportunity to shoot with guys from a wide range of law enforcement agencies and foreign special operations units. This opened the door for me to a wide range of techniques, but I still considered myself an average shooter (among this peer group).

After my third (military) deployment to Iraq, the ATBN was disbanded and I was honorably discharged from active duty as a captain, with my understanding of gunfighting skills and training refined by a few real-world gunfights.

In the civilian world I went to work as a consultant. I provided "operational support" to the US government in Afghanistan and elsewhere. I provided firearms and tactics training to a wide array of US government agencies for personnel with several different missions. I found that my shooting skills were generally at the top end of the SWAT operators I was training across the country, but an unexpected event caused me to re-examine my skill and training.

Each of the agencies I supported had its' own firearms standards. One had standards that were somewhat challenging. In retrospect, I place them as being more demanding than any of the LEAs I had worked with and comparable to some of the pre-deployment standards for various Special Operations Force elements: Doable, but challenging and unforgiving. I fired my qualification course of fire and failed.

I was stunned. I was never the weak link. I spent a few seconds reviewing every excuse I could think of. Then I realized I had only one option. Raise my game, and get my edge back. I spent several days getting dialed back in with USPSA champion Ted Puente in central Florida. We burned through a few thousand rounds and talked throughout. I realized I had let my edge dull. I was sometimes capable of shooting the most demanding standards and sometimes not. That was no good for staying alive and that was no good for staying employed.

With my edge sharpened, I now shoot that same qualification every month to demonstrate to myself that it is no challenge. I now have a very deliberate method for sustainment training. Since then I have continued to provide operational support and train US government personnel.

In recent years, I have had daily use of client ranges and some clients that have provided use of significant quantities of ammo. Work has provided the opportunity to shoot with World Speed Shooting Champion Max Michel, IPSC legend Manny Bragg and many of the guys from the gun mags. I have the pleasure of working with shooters from tier-one special operations units.

The bottom line is this. I have more precision than the average shooter and I have more speed than the average shooter, but I am an unremarkable shooter. I have made shots that my life has

depended on, but I have never competed in any of the shooting sports for score and placement. I have examined the micro-details of the best I had access to. I reviewed the best advice I have ever received. What I can share with you is the best I have been exposed to. Anything that I have done, you can do.

I finally accepted that there is no shortcut. I accept that there is no way to cheat your way to skill. You either take the actions necessary to retain the edge of being able to shoot your best anytime, under any circumstance, or you can expect to shoot your worst when you need it most.

Now I exercise the self-discipline to act on the one piece of guidance I was never willing to do; what I could have done as a 20-year-old Force Reconnaissance Marine. The 30-10 pistol program can do this for you.

BEFORE TRAINING, BEFORE SHOOTING

1) Treat all firearms as if they are loaded.
   a. Even guns that you believe are unloaded.
2) Never let the muzzle of a firearm cover anything that you are not willing to destroy.
   a. This could be another person, a part of your own body, a piece of critical gear, etc.
3) Keep your finger off the trigger and outside of the trigger guard until your sights are aligned on target and you have made the decision to fire.
   a. You must ensure that your finger is not in a position to fire when you have not decided to, even by involuntary spasm such as you might encounter when stumbling, being startled or bumped.
4) Be certain of your target and aware of the environment around it and behind it.
   a. If your round went through the target, where would it go?
   b. If you miss left, right, above or below what is in danger?
   c. Is there anyone likely to get in the way in front of the target?
   d. Are you 100% certain you have acquired the correct target and it is appropriate to fire?
      i. Accidentally shooting your neighbor's target is unacceptable.
      ii. Don't be the idiot hunter who shoots a person, because he 'thought he was a deer'.

Memorize these rules. Live by them. If you do, you will never shoot yourself or someone that is inappropriate to shoot. Firearms training can be dangerous. Gunfighting is dangerous. If you're an adult, not a criminal and you are not mentally deficient, you may choose to legally own a pistol to supplement your ability to defend yourself. You are personally responsible for complying with all relevant laws in your jurisdiction and you are personally responsible for every round fired through your weapon.

SKILLS

The firearm is only one tool in your defense planning. First, you need to sharpen your ability to avoid trouble. Can you predict when, where, how, and with whom you may have trouble? Don't walk into that ambush. If you were targeting yourself, when, where and how would you strike? Do you have the mental, and physical ability, and fitness level necessary to defend yourself empty-handed or with improvised weapons if necessary? If you need improvement in this area see my friends Tim Larkin at www.TargetFocusTraining.com and Andy Curtiss at www.knife-and-h2h-combat.com.

Do you have the mental ability to decide to deliberately do grave harm to another human being in order save your own life? Do you have the ability to rapidly choose between fleeing, fighting and gunfighting and instantly re-evaluate as is morally, and legally appropriate to the circumstance?

Do you consider yourself clumsy, indecisive or inattentive? If yes, then do not buy, possess or handle a firearm.

If you wish to develop skill with a pistol, there is no replacement for competent, live one-on-one instruction. As it says on the back cover of this book, "this does not replace live instruction, this training regimen is a supplement."

If you are a police officer, your basic police academy training should be sufficient to start this program. If you are in the US military and received GOOD pistol training, including: safety, marksmanship, loading, unloading, draw- stroke, immediate action, and remedial action, your training should be sufficient to start this program.

If you have any doubts about the quality of instruction you have received, feel that a warm-up would be beneficial, or have not received training, you will need to exercise initiative and get your own.

If you live on the East Coast, you may want to attend a pistol course with Jeff Gonzales (www.tridentconcepts.com). If you're on the West Coast you may want to train with Max Joseph (www.tftt.com). If you are in the south I highly recommend Greg Lapin (www.vatatrainingcenter.com).

Regardless, you need a high-quality two or three day pistol course under your belt to start. There is a huge number of shooting instructors out there. There's a decent number of GOOD shooting instructors out there. Be judicious.

In this manual, you will find discussion of fundamentals. When you attend a course, shoot the entire course with the techniques the instructor advocates. When the course is done, you may evaluate what is and is not appropriate to retain; however, if you did not execute exactly as was advocated, you are not making an assessment of the instructor's techniques, you are judging your own bastardized version of his technique. When you shoot with a more skilled shooter than yourself, and you find yourself saying, "that's not comfortable for me" or "I prefer to do it this way", you are most likely identifying some of the reasons why your shooting is inferior to his.

You will inevitably find some minor variation in this manual from what your instructor taught. Use whichever technique is most appropriate for your actual mission and circumstance.

PRECISION

Do not be sloppy! Be precise! In every repetition you perform, be as precise in each micro-detail as is humanly possible. Make every press of the trigger perfect practice. Two perfect repetitions is better than 100 good. Go as slow as is comfortable to execute perfectly and only add speed incrementally after perfection is achieved. Accelerate your repetitions until you commit errors, then slow it down and execute perfectly. Push the envelope a little farther each time.

Get in the habit of executing each drill to completion before resetting. A week from now that may mean coming from the holster and making one perfect dry fire shot without resetting even though you partially grabbed a handful of cover- garment (e.g. an open button down shirt) on the way to the holster. In the field this might be the difference between executing an efficient immediate action drill and firing accurate shots, saving your life rather than pausing or hesitating and being shot.

Also, you'll get the best results if you attend a GOOD pistol course and begin this 30 day regimen immediately after completion of that course. It is highly recommended that you conduct NO live- fire, Sim-fire, Airsoft or paintball DURING this 30 day program.

NOTE: It is recommended that you conduct all 30 15 minute training sessions over a 30 day period with no days off.

NOTE: If you choose to conduct two lessons in one day, it is recommended that you divide the two lessons with an entirely separate task such as a workout, running errands, etc.

NOTE: High-level shooting skills require precise execution of hundreds of micro-skills. These skills are extremely perishable.

EQUIPMENT

You will need your duty rig. After the concealment shirt is introduced in training, wear your weapon as you wear it for work. If you are a civilian and do not have a duty setup mandated by your agency, you'll have to get your own and you can follow the drills exactly. If you are purchasing, you may want to look at a Glock 9 x 19 mm (17 or 19) as you prefer. Glocks are generally rugged, reliable, and perform well out-of-the-box (not all firearms do). 9 x 19 mm (Parabellum, Luger or NATO, etc.) is probably the smallest (and cheapest!) caliber to deliberately carry for defense.

NOTE: Shooting a person once with .45 ACP may be more effective than shooting him or her (in the same spot) with a 9 x 19 mm, however, for individuals wrapped around the axle on this let me share the comment of a friend. "Monkey", A SEAL friend that was teaching a class of federal law-enforcement agents with me told one class: "statistics show that the majority of people shot with a pistol survive. Statistics also show that 100% of people that were shot with a 9 mm by me are dead." This quip illustrates the importance of accuracy and speed over caliber.

Glocks are simpler to operate than a single action pistol (e.g. 1911 or Browning Hi-Power). Thumb movement to deactivate a safety is not necessary.

They are more efficient to train with than double action pistols (e.g. Beretta 92 or Sig P226). A double action shooter must master two separate trigger pulls and have situational awareness on every shot whether it is a heavy or lighter press (of the trigger).

A Glock shooter has one trigger pressure to master. He gets twice the training benefit of the double action shooter with the same amount of ammo.

So you need a pistol, three magazines, a suitable holster, double magazine pouch (see Tactical Products Group, SOTech, Bladetech, Fobus, etc. for holsters and pouches if you need one) and a suitable belt. You will need a single-hand operated white light (such as a SureFire, etc.) with a pouch. You will need sunglasses, and three magazines full of dummy (non-firing, non-operational, training) rounds that are the same caliber as your pistol.

When positioning your holster there are a few considerations. It is generally most quickly accessed slightly forward of the hip. This also flares the grip out for easy access. Unfortunately it can inhibit leg movement when squatting and is generally not easy to keep concealed. Behind the hip generally provides better concealment, but slows access. You must confirm your gear is accessible. Decide where it will best serve you and keep it consistent.

WARNING: You will need a safe room for training. The backstop (wall) must be capable of stopping a negligently discharged round. There must be NO live ammo anywhere in this room or anywhere on the trainee. Access to the room must be controlled so that there is no risk of anyone unexpectedly walking into the room.

You'll need a shot timer. You'll need a functioning television in the safe room with an appropriate backstop. You will need point targets such as nickel-sized colored sticker disks, colored thumbtacks, an IPSC target, a tennis ball and approximately 10' of string. You will need a video camera.

CAUTION: You will notice that the demo shooter photographed is wearing cargo pants, a tactical vest, etc. A good tactical vest is well designed to aid shooter maneuvering, but is easily recognizable anywhere in the world as a likely concealment garment. Do all training in every day shirts and jackets. As you're going through the course, don't hold yourself accountable for techniques that haven't been specifically mentioned. As an example, on the pictures show different support hand grips (thumbs forward vs. not) early on in the course, but you don't need to do anything specific with your support hand grip until it is specifically addressed.

NOTE: SureFire has a free shot timer app for iPhone users.

STOP: If you have not attended high quality, LIVE pistol SAFETY instruction such as may be obtained from your **local NRA certified instructor DO NOT CONTINUE until you do!**

©2013

C. Graham

DAY 1: MARKSMANSHIP

WARNING: Treat all firearms as if they are loaded, Never let the muzzle of a firearm cover anything that you are not willing to destroy, Keep your finger off the trigger and outside of the trigger guard until your sights are aligned on target and you have made the decision to fire, Be certain of your target and aware of the environment around it and behind it!

WARNING: Confirm each round loaded is a non-firing dummy and that there are no live rounds anywhere in the training room.

DRILL 1:
WHICH EYE IS DOMINANT?

1.A Sight Alignment

- Note start time

- Stand on the opposite side of a room from a light switch

- Ensure your head is straight toward the switch

- Ensure your shoulders are each equidistant from the switch

- Hold one thumb at arms length between you and the switch

- Close the left eye, if the switch is directly behind your thumb, you are right eye dominant

- Close the right eye, if the switch is directly behind your thumb, you are left eye dominant

- This can be done with either thumb

See Image 1.A

NOTE: Sight Alignment= the tip of the front sight centered from left to right in the rear sights and flush across the top of the rear sight. This generally provides a more precise shot than focusing on any images painted on the sights.

See Image 1.B

NOTE: Sight Picture= perfectly aligned sights with the front sight tip superimposed over the intended point of impact.

DRILL 2:
SIGHT ALIGNMENT & SIGHT PICTURE

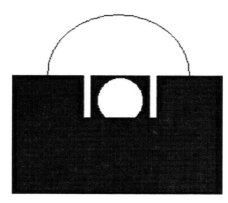

1.B Sight Picture

- Place a colored thumbtack on the wall (your target) on cardboard or corkboard etc.

- Load all three magazines to capacity WITH DUMMY NON-FIRING ROUNDS ONLY

- Stand 6' from the target

- All movements today should be SLOW

- Load one magazine of Dummy rounds and chamber a DUMMY round by bringing the slide to the rear limit with the non-firing hand and releasing it

CAUTION: Riding the slide forward instead of releasing it can induce malfunctions.

- Using both hands, hold the pistol directly in front of your dominant eye, oriented to the target with perfect sight alignment and perfect sight picture, your point of focus is the tip of the front sight

NOTE: Shooting while breathing will be inconsistent. Immediately pause breathing (no need to gulp or hold breath) while shooting.

CAUTION: Do not lower your head, raise the pistol to eye level.

NOTE: Shooting with both eyes open is a huge advantage. If you currently close an eye to shoot, this 30 day program is the perfect opportunity to break that habit. SHOOT BOTH EYES OPEN FOR EVERY SESSION! If this is currently undoable, squint your non-dominant eye on Day 1. Wean yourself of this day by day. Execute the drills with both eyes open by day 5 and continue both eyes open.

- Operate the trigger by smoothly pressuring straight to the rear without disturbing sight alignment and sight picture NOTE: Find the spot on your trigger finger that can operate the trigger as straight as possible to the rear.

CAUTION: Too much finger will push the trigger diagonally in one direction, too little, the other. Use the same optimal position for every shot.

- Once you have "broken the shot" on a dummy round, confirm sight alignment and sight picture are perfect and use the non-firing hand to operate the slide again chambering the next dummy round NOTE: Continue to hold the trigger finger in the exact position that "broke the shot", do not add or release pressure yet.

CAUTION: disturbing the sights microscopically while firing will throw off a shot a little bit at close range and yards at distance.

- Place your non firing hand back on the weapon just as you want it, reconfirm sight picture and reset the trigger by easing forward the trigger finger ONLY ENOUGH to feel the reset

NOTE: Build the habit of operating the trigger just far enough to break the shot and just far enough forward to reset.

CAUTION: Excess movement of the trigger finger and slapping or jerking will throw rounds off even at close range.

- Continue this process for each remaining round in that magazine

- Each round is a perfect shot. Call each. Did it break left, down etc? Smooth pressure. Break perfectly without ratcheting or halting.

NOTE: The trigger finger MUST operate the trigger without contacting the frame anywhere throughout operation.

CAUTION: Scraping the frame above or below the trigger inside the trigger guard while operating the trigger will throw shots off- a small amount at close range, yards at distance.

VIDEO – 1.A STAGED TRIGGER SHOT AND RESET

HTTP://TACTICSANDPREPAREDNESS.COM/3010-1A

DRILL 3:
SIGHT PICTURE AND GRIP

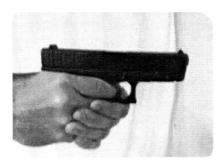

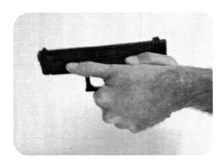

1.C & 1.D Grip

- Load a fresh magazine of DUMMY ROUNDS ONLY and chamber a Dummy round as before

- Acquire perfect sight picture

- Mentally focus on grip

See Images 1.C & 1.D

- The firing hand should by high on the pistol grip (without interfering with slide function)

NOTE: The pistol should be held securely by the two middle fingers of the shooting hand without disturbing aim. Pinky can be relaxed.

Trigger finger MUST move independently of any sympathetic movement in any other finger!

NOTE: Developing a strong grip now and using it consistently for every shot, starting right at the time of grasping the weapon will be a great advantage in recoil control for multiple fast shots in future shooting.

- The non-firing hand should wrap around the grip, with thumbs stacked as pictured

- The non-firing hand forms a solid base, firing hand applies steady pressure, locking forward into the non-firing hand

- Trigger finger is moved completely independently of tension in the other fingers/pressure in the hands holding the weapon tight

- Dry-fire each DUMMY round in the magazine perfectly as in Drill 2

- Be consistent

DRILL 4:
SIGHT PICTURE, GRIP, ISOSCELES

- Load your third magazine of DUMMY rounds and chamber one

- Ensure that your hips are exactly equidistant to the target

- Ensure that your shoulders form the two points of a triangle with the target as the third point

- Roll your center of gravity forward. You should not be leaning back, you should not be standing straight up and down

NOTE: Most good shooters extend their arms fully, locking elbows, with elbows facing out (not down).

- Execute Drill 2 and Drill 3 perfectly for each DUMMY round in this magazine

DRILL 5:
REPEAT

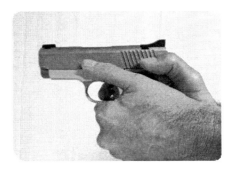

1.E Grip 1911 (Single Action)

1.F Grip Smith (Double Action)

- Load all three magazines with three DUMMY rounds each
- Repeat Drill 2 for one magazine
- Repeat Drill 3 for one magazine
- Repeat Drill 4 for one magazine

- Repeat Drill 5 for duration of time

- Note time

IF DRY-FIRING A SINGLE ACTION PISTOL, the shooting hand thumb is positioned on the safety. The thumb must place the safety on fire for each series of shots. The drills begin with a magazine of DUMMY rounds loaded, a DUMMY round in the chamber, the hammer back and safety on. The same thumb places the weapon on safe each time the string of dry-fire is concluded. There is no benefit to being too hasty to place the safety back on.

See Image 1.E Grip 1911 (Single Action)

IF DRY-FIRING A DOUBLE ACTION PISTOL, The thumb must place the safety on fire for each series of shots. The drills begin with a magazine of DUMMY rounds loaded, a DUMMY round in the chamber, the hammer de-cocked (down) and safety on. The same thumb de-cocks/places the weapon on safe each time the string of dry-fire is concluded. This photo depicts the shooter having taken the safety off, pressuring the trigger to the rear to break a dry-fire shot and the hammer can be seen moving to the rear. For each drill practiced in 30-10 dry-fire two shots; The first double action (hammer down), the second single action (hammer back).

See Image 1.F Grip Smith (Double Action)

LOG: Begin a 30 day log. What do you most want to remember from today?

QUESTION OF THE DAY: What did you do today that is different from your previous shooting techniques?

DAY 2: PRESENT THE WEAPON

WARNING: Treat all firearms as if they are loaded, Never let the muzzle of a firearm cover anything that you are not willing to destroy, Keep your finger off the trigger and outside of the trigger guard until your sights are aligned on target and you have made the decision to fire, Be certain of your target and aware of the environment around it and behind it!

WARNING: Confirm each round loaded is a non-firing dummy and that there are no live rounds anywhere in the training room.

Note: Review your Log entries from yesterday.

DRILL 1:
ENGAGE FROM THE LOW READY

- Note start time
- Place a colored thumbtack on the wall (your target) on cardboard or corkboard etc
- Load all three magazines to capacity WITH DUMMY NON-FIRING ROUNDS ONLY
- Stand 5' from the target
- All movements today should be SLOW
- Load one magazine of Dummy rounds and chamber a DUMMY round by bringing the slide to the rear limit with the non-firing hand and releasing it
- Confirm both feet are approximately shoulder width apart (or a little wider)

- The foot on your shooting-hand side can be a couple inches to a few inches toward the rear as in a fighting stance Ensure that your hips are exactly equidistant to the target

See Image 2.A Stance

- Ensure that your shoulders form the two points of a triangle with the target as the third point

- Roll your center of gravity forward, you should not be leaning back, you should not be standing straight up and down

See Image 2.B Low Ready

- Begin at the low ready for each dry-fire shot

2.A Stance

2.B Low Ready

NOTE: This position is useful for tasks such as room clearing, etc.

- Trigger finger begins along the slide.

- Using all the techniques from DAY 1 Marksmanship dry-fire each DUMMY round of the first magazine perfectly

NOTE: Confirm site picture as pressuring the trigger, as "breaking the shot" and after the shot before cycling the next Dummy round.

DRILL 2:
ENGAGE FROM POSITION SUL

- Stand 5' from the target

- All movements are SLOW

- Load one magazine of DUMMY rounds and chamber a DUMMY round by bringing the slide to the rear limit with the non-firing hand and releasing it

See Image 2.C Sul

NOTE: Special thanks to Max Joseph for position Sul.

- Ensure that your hips are exactly equidistant to the target

- Ensure that your shoulders form the two points of a triangle with the target as the third point

- Roll your center of gravity forward, you should not be leaning back, you should not be standing straight up and down

- Begin at position Sul for each dry-fire shot

2.C Sul

NOTE: This position is useful in a "stack" with teammates in front of you, when pivoting past a teammate or when a teammate begins to step in front of your muzzle.

Using all the techniques from DAY 1 Marksmanship fire each DUMMY round of this magazine perfectly

DRILL 3:
PRESENT FROM THE READY

2.D Ready

- Stand 5' from the target

- All movements are SLOW

- Load one magazine of Dummy rounds and chamber a DUMMY round by bringing the slide to the rear limit with the non-firing hand and releasing it

See Image 2.D Ready

- Ensure that your hips are exactly equidistant to the target

- Ensure that your shoulders form the two points of a triangle with the target as the third point

- Roll your center of gravity forward, you should not be leaning back, you should not be standing straight up and down

VIDEO – 2.A READY TO PRESENTATION

HTTP://TACTICSANDPREPAREDNESS.COM/3010-2A

- Begin at the Ready position for each dry-fire shot

NOTE: This position is useful in room clearing when the weapon must be drawn closer to the body to negotiate obstacles, when a close range closing aggressor may access your fully projected pistol or as the intermediate stage of a drawstroke.

- Bring the pistol to eye level and project straight toward the intended point of impact on the target, you should be acquiring the front sight tip and confirming sight picture at the earliest possible moment

NOTE: Some shooters find it helpful to visualize the correct motion by imagining a model train track in front of your dominant eye. You are raising the pistol up to the track, then sliding it straight down the track toward the target.

NOTE: As soon as the sights are aligned with the target and you have decided that it is appropriate and necessary to fire, your trigger finger should be pressing the trigger, removing slack.

WARNING: It is possible to break an accurate shot at any time during presentation from the ready. How fast the sight picture will be confirmed is based on: size and distance of the target and your speed in picking up the front sight tip (visually).

- Using all the techniques from DAY 1 Marksmanship dry-fire each DUMMY round perfectly

DRILL 4:
REPEAT

- Load all three magazines with three DUMMY rounds each

- Repeat Drill 1 for one magazine

- Repeat Drill 2 for one magazine

- Repeat Drill 3 for one magazine

- Repeat Drill 4 for duration of time

- Note time

IF YOU ARE DRY-FIRING A SINGLE ACTION PISTOL, the safe will come off and any slack can be taken out of the trigger when the decision to dry-fire has been made and the sights are aligned to the target (the weapon may still be being projected forward toward the target). The shot is broken when the shooter confirms the front sight is positioned as desired and the shooter is ready to fire.

IF YOU ARE DRY-FIRING A DOUBLE ACTION PISTOL, the safe will come off and the trigger is "staged" (pressed toward "threshold" without "breaking" the shot), when the decision to fire has been made and the sights are aligned to the target (the weapon may still be being projected forward toward the target). The shot is broken when the shooter confirms the front sight is positioned as desired and the shooter is ready to fire. For each drill practiced in 30-10 dry-fire two shots; The first double action (hammer down), the second single action (hammer back).

VIDEO – 2.B DOUBLE ACTION PRESENT FROM READY

HTTP://TACTICSANDPREPAREDNESS.COM/3010-2B

LOG: What do you most want to retain from today?

QUESTION OF THE DAY: If criminals are willing to kill with firearms, why do activists believe that killers would abide by laws banning the sale or ownership of firearms?

DAY 3: FROM THE HOLSTER

WARNING: Treat all firearms as if they are loaded, Never let the muzzle of a firearm cover anything that you are not willing to destroy, Keep your finger off the trigger and outside of the trigger guard until your sights are aligned on target and you have made the decision to fire, Be certain of your target and aware of the environment around it and behind it!

WARNING: Confirm each round loaded is a non-firing dummy and that there are no live rounds anywhere in the training room.

Note: Review your Log entries from yesterday.

DRILL 1:
FROM THE HOLSTER

- Note start time

- Place a nickel sized colored sticker on the wall (your target)

- Load all three magazines to capacity WITH DUMMY NON-FIRING ROUNDS ONLY

- Stand 6' from the target

- All movements today should be SLOW

- Load one magazine of Dummy rounds and chamber a DUMMY round by bringing the slide to the rear limit with the non-firing hand and releasing it

- Start with the non-firing hand pressed to the chest and the firing-hand already gripping the holstered pistol perfectly

- The firing hand moves the weapon to clear the holster

3.A From The Holster

NOTE: On some holsters this is straight up, some holsters have a forward cant, some are adjustable.

NOTE: If your holster has a thumb break or other retaining device, you will need to use the most efficient deactivation motion possible consistently for every drawstroke. Use the retaining device on every drawstroke practiced.

CAUTION: Moving extra, unnecessary distance is inefficient and wastes time.

- The firing hand rotates the muzzle to point at the target immediately upon clearing the holster

- The firing hand moves in the most direct route to link up with the non-firing hand at center chest forming the Ready Position

- Using all the techniques from DAY 1 Marksmanship and Day 2

- Present the Weapon/Ready Position dry-fire each DUMMY round of three magazines perfectly from the holster

NOTE: Eye focus should be concentrated on a precise point of aim on the target. The shooter should transition focus to the tip of the front sight tip as the tip enters the line of sight and keep focus on the tip until all shooting is completed.

CAUTION: Transitioning focus back and forth more times than is necessary between the target and front sight tip costs time and is inefficient.

DRILL 2:
REPEAT

- Load all three magazines to capacity with DUMMY rounds

- Repeat Drill 1 for duration of time

- Note time

VIDEO – 3.A DRAWSTROKE TO SHOT

HTTP://TACTICSANDPREPAREDNESS.COM/3010-3A

LOG: Enter what you do not wish to forget about this session.

QUESTION OF THE DAY: What was yesterday's first WARNING?

DAY 4: THE DRAWSTROKE

WARNING: Treat all firearms as if they are loaded, Never let the muzzle of a firearm cover anything that you are not willing to destroy, Keep your finger off the trigger and outside of the trigger guard until your sights are aligned on target and you have made the decision to fire, Be certain of your target and aware of the environment around it and behind it!

WARNING: Confirm each round loaded is a non-firing dummy and that there are no live rounds anywhere in the training room.

DRILL 1:
THE DRAWSTROKE

4.A Hands At Sides

- Note start time
- Place a nickel sized colored sticker on the wall (your target)

- Load all three magazines to capacity WITH DUMMY NON-FIRING ROUNDS ONLY

- Stand 7' from the target

- Movements should be SLOW

- Load one magazine of Dummy rounds and chamber a DUMMY round by bringing the slide to the rear limit with the non-firing hand and releasing it

- Start with foot position and body position in your perfect shooting stance

- Start with both hands relaxed at your sides

Image 4.A Hands At Sides

- The firing hand curls into a hook (with the thumb out of the way).

NOTE: Both hands move simultaneously!

NOTE: Do not lean (to the side) when accessing the holster. If this is necessary, your holster is either poorly positioned or poorly designed.

WARNING: Moving hands incorrectly could result in the non-firing hand getting in front of the muzzle. THAT IS A VIOLATION OF THE FOUR SAFETY RULES!

- The non-firing hand moves on the most direct route to center chest, while simultaneously the firing hand moves upward, lifting the pistol and rolling the thumb into position for a perfect grip while the pistol is moving toward the top of the holster

- Using all the techniques from Day 1 Marksmanship, Day 2 Present the Weapon/ Ready Position and Day 3 From the Holster, fire each DUMMY round of three magazines perfectly beginning with hands relaxed at the sides

DRILL 2:
REPEAT

- Load all three magazines with three DUMMY rounds each

- Repeat Drill 1 adding speed after each magazine is dry-fired

- Note time

- Repeat the drill perfectly using three magazines of three DUMMY rounds each moving as SLOWLY as is humanly possible

IF YOU ARE DRY-FIRING A SINGLE ACTION PISTOL, the safe will come off and any slack can be taken out of the trigger when the decision to dry-fire has been made and the sights are aligned to the target (this might be immediately after clearing the holster). The shot is broken when the shooter confirms the front sight is positioned as desired and the shooter is ready to fire.

IF YOU ARE DRY-FIRING A DOUBLE ACTION PISTOL, the safe will come off and the trigger is "staged" (pressed toward "threshold" without "breaking" the shot) when the decision to fire has been made and the sights are aligned to the target (this might be immediately after clearing the holster). The shot is broken when the shooter confirms the front sight is positioned as desired and the shooter is ready to fire. For each drill practiced in 30-10 dry-fire two shots; The first double action (hammer down), the second single action (hammer back) for each drill repetition.

VIDEO 4.A – DRAWSTROKE AND TRIGGER RESET

HTTP://TACTICSANDPREPAREDNESS.COM/3010-4A

LOG: Make your entries.

QUESTION OF THE DAY: Since courts have recognized that no law enforcement agency can be held responsible for your (personal) protection or that of your family members, who is responsible for your security?

DAY 5: THE DRAWSTROKE FROM CONCEALMENT (BUTTON DOWN)

WARNING: Treat all firearms as if they are loaded, Never let the muzzle of a firearm cover anything that you are not willing to destroy, Keep your finger off the trigger and outside of the trigger guard until your sights are aligned on target and you have made the decision to fire, Be certain of your target and aware of the environment around it and behind it!

WARNING: Confirm each round loaded is a non-firing dummy and that there are no live rounds anywhere in the training room.

NOTE: Review your Log entries from yesterday.

DRILL 1:
DRAWSTROKE FROM (OPEN) BUTTON DOWN SHIRT (OR OPEN JACKET)

- Note start time

- Place a nickel sized colored sticker on the wall (your target)

- Load all three magazines to capacity WITH DUMMY NON-FIRING ROUNDS ONLY

- Stand 6' from the target

- Movements should be SLOW

- Load one magazine of Dummy rounds and chamber a DUMMY round by bringing the slide to the rear limit with the non-firing hand and releasing it

5.A Interview Position

- Start with foot position and body position in your perfect shooting stance

- Start with both hands in the "interview position"

See Image 5.A Interview Position

NOTE: The purpose of the interview position is to position your hands for efficient use to block, fight, or draw your pistol (when in a mildly elevated level of alert.)

NOTE: Interview Position is intended to be done in such a way that it projects your intent to others as minimally as possible.

WARNING: Laced fingers may be easy for an opponent to trap.

WARNING: Moving hands incorrectly could result in the non-firing hand getting in front of the muzzle. THAT IS A VIOLATION OF THE FOUR SAFETY RULES!

VIDEO 5.A – DRAWSTROKE CONCEALED

HTTP://TACTICSANDPREPAREDNESS.COM/3010-5A

5.B Draw From Concealment

- The non-firing hand moves on the most direct route to center chest, while simultaneously the firing hand moves in a knife edge motion flinging the shirt open (this motion can only be done successfully fast)

NOTE: Momentum accelerates the cover garment out of the way as the firing hand changes direction and moves directly to the pistol.

- Using all the techniques from Day 1 Marksmanship, Day 2 Present the Weapon/ Ready Position, Day 3 From the Holster, and Day 4 Drawstroke fire each DUMMY round of three magazines perfectly from concealment

DRILL 2:
REPEAT

- Load all three magazines with three DUMMY rounds each

- Repeat Drill 1 adding speed after each magazine is dry-fired

- Note time

- Repeat the drill perfectly using one magazine of three DUMMY rounds moving as SLOWLY as is humanly possible (not including the flinging of the cover garment) for each

VIDEO – 5.B REHOLSTER

HTTP://TACTICSANDPREPAREDNESS.COM/3010-5B

LOG: Make your entries.

QUESTION OF THE DAY: When do you begin applying pressure to the trigger?

DAY 6: LOAD AND UNLOAD

WARNING: Treat all firearms as if they are loaded, Never let the muzzle of a firearm cover anything that you are not willing to destroy, Keep your finger off the trigger and outside of the trigger guard until your sights are aligned on target and you have made the decision to fire, Be certain of your target and aware of the environment around it and behind it!

WARNING: Confirm each round loaded is a non-firing dummy and that there are no live rounds anywhere in the training room.

NOTE: Review your Log entries from yesterday.

DRILL 1:
LOAD

6.A Load position

- Note start time

- Place a nickel sized colored sticker on the wall (your target)

- Load three magazines with three DUMMY NON-FIRING ROUNDS each

- Stand 5' from the target

- Wear gunbelt with open button down shirt or open jacket for concealment

NOTE: It is recommended that you use several different concealment garments for training.

WARNING: Never wear a concealment garment on operations that you have not trained in.

- Movements should be SLOW

- Present your empty pistol to the target in a perfect drawstroke

CAUTION: You will not pressure the trigger, or place your finger on the trigger, because you have NOT decided that it is appropriate to attempt to fire.

- Confirm there is NO magazine in the weapon

- Using the palm and four fingers of the non- firing hand, lock the slide to the rear

- Keeping the weapon oriented in a safe direction (down-range in this case) visually inspect the weapon through the ejection port

NOTE: You are confirming that there is NO ammo, debris or damage in the chamber or anyplace visible.

NOTE: You are making a mental note of the level of cleanliness and lubrication visible

CAUTION: Some instructors encourage physically inspecting the chamber (sticking a finger in). I do not. Fingers in weapons can be injured. Fingers in larger weapons (e.g. machineguns) can be crushed.

- When your inspection is complete, bring the pistol to the Load position with the firing hand

See Image 6.A Load position

NOTE: This position must be between the eyes and the horizon so that your peripheral vision will maintain your awareness of movement and conditions in front of you.

CAUTION: Holding the pistol low will maintain situational awareness on the ground in front of you, allowing people to maneuver in front of you without your awareness.

6.B Accessing a magazine pouch (note finger position)

- Simultaneously, the non-firing hand follows the most direct route under the shirt and accesses the front magazine in the magazine pouch

See Image 6.B Accessing a magazine pouch (note finger position)

NOTE: Always carry magazines projectile forward.

NOTE: Always carry the best magazine (e.g. most full) in the front.

NOTE: Index finger is on the tip of the top round.

6.C Firmly seat the mag

- Withdraw the magazine from the pouch, orient it toward the pistol and follow the most direct route to the pistol with the non-firing hand.

See Image 6.C Firmly seat the mag

- Firmly seat the magazine

- The non-firing hand thumb sweeps the slide release, as a backup, the firing hand thumb then sweeps the slide release as both hands are coming together with thumbs stacked for a perfect grip

- Simultaneously, the weapon is rotated back on target

- The weapon is pushed straight forward to the desired extension

- Fire three perfect dry-fire shots

CAUTION: Some manufacturers advocate not operating the slide with this technique. Defer to the manufacturers recommendation.

DRILL:
2 UNLOAD

NOTE: On your last dry-fire shot, the slide will lock to the rear when it is moved there, this is the position of a pistol fired until out of ammo.

- Rotate the weapon to the Load Postion (above)

- Press the magazine release with the firing hand thumb

- Catch the ejected magazine with the non-firing hand at the base of the pistol grip

NOTE: Make gravity work for you, not against you. Orient the weapon such that gravity will pull the magazine out.

CAUTION: Using the non-firing hand to pull the magazine out is a training scar. This will result in habitually inefficient magazine changes. If the magazine CAN NOT fall freely from the weapon, have the weapon inspected by an armorer/gunsmith.

- Place the empty magazine in a pocket

CAUTION: Do not store empty mags in a mag pouch with full mags or in the same pocket as partially loaded mags.

WARNING: If the pistol were loaded when beginning 'Unload', the slide would be forward and the process would be the same WITH THE ADDITION of moving the slide to the rear with the non-firing hand palm and four fingers AFTER the magazine was removed. This would eject the chambered round.

NOTE: Let ejected rounds fall, do not chase them or attempt to catch.

- Re-form a perfect grip and project to perfect presentation of the weapon

- Once you have fired a perfect dry-fire shot or decided not to fire (as appropriate to your agency and circumstance) return to the Ready Postion

- With the weapon steady and unmoving, slowly scan as far behind you as possible, and do the same in the opposite direction

NOTE: You are developing a scanning habit to determine if it is safe/appropriate to re-holster.

NOTE: There is no benefit to re-holstering speed; take your time.

- If the environment is clear and you wish to re- holster, use the non-firing hand (travelling behind the pistol) to lift the shirt flap out of the way

- Once that is done, bring the firing-hand and pistol back from the Ready to the holster in the reverse track of a perfect drawstroke

NOTE: Develop the habit of doing this with focus down-range not looking at your holster.

NOTE: Once the pistol is vertical to reinsert in the holster, the firing hand thumb should continuously apply pressure to the back of the slide until re-holstering is complete.

CAUTION: If the slide is not held forward with the firing hand thumb it is possible to knock some pistols out of battery on the lip of the holster.

DRILL 3:
REPEAT

- Ensure all three magazines are loaded with three DUMMY rounds each

- Repeat Drill 1 dry-firing three Dummy rounds perfectly, then repeat Drill 2

- Repeat the drills perfectly using three magazines of three DUMMY rounds each for remaining time

- Note time

IF YOU ARE DRY-FIRING A SINGLE ACTION PISTOL, ensure that the safety has been placed on prior to holstering.

IF YOU ARE DRY-FIRING A DOUBLE ACTION PISTOL, ensure that the weapon has been de-cocked prior to holstering.

VIDEO – 6.A LOAD

HTTP://TACTICSANDPREPAREDNESS.COM/3010-6A

VIDEO 6.B UNLOAD

HTTP://TACTICSANDPREPAREDNESS.COM/3010-6B

LOG: Make your entries.

QUESTION OF THE DAY: Why would it be appropriate for a police officer to use effective weapons when attempting to apprehend a violent home- invasion crew, but only acceptable for a citizen to defend herself against the same vicious criminals with an inferior weapon to that of the police officer?

DAY 7: COMBAT RELOAD

WARNING: Treat all firearms as if they are loaded, Never let the muzzle of a firearm cover anything that you are not willing to destroy, Keep your finger off the trigger and outside of the trigger guard until your sights are aligned on target and you have made the decision to fire, Be certain of your target and aware of the environment around it and behind it!

WARNING: Confirm each round loaded is a non-firing dummy and that there are no live rounds anywhere in the training room.

NOTE: Review your Log entries from yesterday.

DRILL 1:
COMBAT RELOAD (DRAWSTROKE FROM OPEN BUTTON DOWN SHIRT)

7.A Combat Reload

- Note start time

- Place a nickel sized colored sticker on the wall (your target)

- Load all three magazines with three DUMMY NON-FIRING ROUNDS each

- Stand 6' from the target

- Movements should be SLOW

- Load one magazine of Dummy rounds and return to the holster

- Start with both hands relaxed at your sides

- Slowly execute perfect dry-fire shots from the holster

NOTE: If you have decided to fire and the sights are aligned on target, you should be pressuring the slack out of the trigger during the drawstroke.

- After each dry-fire shot, follow through and confirm sites are still perfectly centered on your intended point of impact

- Then cycle the weapon with the non-firing hand while holding the trigger in place

- Once your perfect grip is re-established, training resumes, release the trigger far enough forward to reset the trigger only

CAUTION: Moving the trigger farther than necessary is inefficient, time consuming, and encourages shooters to "slap" triggers or otherwise shoot sloppily (inaccurately).

- Continue dry-firing slow perfect shots until out of ammo

CAUTION: Do not count rounds. Counting rounds with three round magazines may be practical, but with full magazines and distractions it is not.

- EXECUTE COMBAT RELOAD- firing hand immediately moves to the Load position — non firing hand simultaneously moves to the magazine pouch

- The non-firing hand produces the fresh magazine as the firing hand thumb releases the empty magazine

NOTE: The slide is locked to the rear- empty.

- The empty mag falling and the fresh mag being inserted pass each other in flight

- The non-firing hand thumb sweeps the slide release, the firing hand thumb sweeps the slide release, both thumbs stack and the grip is resumed normally as the weapon is rotated to point at the target and projected straight out

See Image 7.A Combat Reload

VIDEO 7.A – COMBAT RELOAD

HTTP://TACTICSANDPREPAREDNESS.COM/3010-7A

CAUTION: Many firearms instructors teach students to "take a knee" to simulate seeking cover. "Taking a knee" is often not an appropriate way to seek cover. "Taking a knee" at an inopportune time is as detrimental as not moving at all. "Taking a knee" can be a training scar; it is intended to simulate the answer, not be the answer.

NOTE: If a pistol runs dry and the slide does not lock to the rear, finish changing mags and operate the slide as in Load.

NOTE: It is our goal to make Combat Reload automatic and instantaneous anytime a weapon runs dry.

NOTE: It is beneficial to simultaneously take cover when reloading.

NOTE: Concealment is anything that hides you from view; cover is anything that protects you from bullets, blast and fragmentation.

CAUTION: The totality of circumstances will dictate the propriety of taking cover, moving etc. Eg- if you are working with a team your unexpected movement may cause more problems than it solves.

DRILL 2:
REPEAT

NOTE: If operating with teammates it is beneficial to advise them "Gun down" and "Gun up" so they may provide security and temporarily take responsibility for your sector of fire, or create agreed upon brevity codes.

NOTE: If regularly operating with the same teammates it is beneficial to use a brevity code instead of announcing "Gun down" that an adversary might hear.

- Load all three magazines with three DUMMY rounds each

- Repeat Drill 1 adding speed after each magazine is dry-fired

- Note time

- Repeat the drill perfectly using three magazines of three DUMMY rounds each moving as SLOWLY as is humanly possible (not including the flinging of the cover garment)

LOG: Make your entries.

QUESTION OF THE DAY: Why is it important to hold the weapon at eye- level when conducting a Combat Reload?

DAY 8: TACTICAL RELOAD

WARNING: Treat all firearms as if they are loaded, Never let the muzzle of a firearm cover anything that you are not willing to destroy, Keep your finger off the trigger and outside of the trigger guard until your sights are aligned on target and you have made the decision to fire, Be certain of your target and aware of the environment around it and behind it!

WARNING: Confirm each round loaded is a non-firing dummy and that there are no live rounds anywhere in the training room.

NOTE: Review your Log entries from yesterday.

DRILL 1:
TACTICAL RELOAD (DRAWSTROKE FROM OPEN BUTTON DOWN SHIRT)

- Note start time
- Place a nickel sized colored sticker on the wall (your target)
- Load all three magazines to capacity with DUMMY NON-FIRING ROUNDS
- Stand 7' from the target
- Movements should be SLOW
- Load one magazine of Dummy rounds and return to the holster
- Start with both hands relaxed at your sides
- Slowly execute three perfect dry-fire shots from the holster

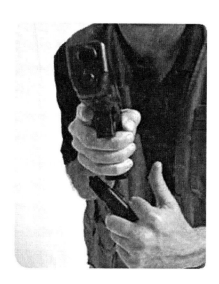

8.A Tac Reload approach with fresh mag

8.B Tac Reload withdraw partial mag and insert fresh mag

NOTE: We are simulating that you have been in an engagement, you have fired rounds, but that there is a lull in the fight, you have cover (ideally you have a teammate providing security) and you have decided to take advantage of the opportunity to load a full magazine.

- With the non-firing hand, access a fresh magazine (as in "Load") and bring it to the pistol

- The pistol should be oriented to the target

See Image 8.A Tac Reload approach with fresh mag

See Image 8.B Tac Reload withdraw partial mag and insert fresh mag

- Execute the tactical reload as pictured

NOTE: Until the magazine is ejected, you have a charged weapon to use. When the mag is ejected you have one round in the chamber that can be fired from most models of pistol. When the fresh mag is inserted, you have the chambered round plus a full magazine.

CAUTION: Minimize time that no mag is in the weapon.

NOTE: The weapon is charged and stays charged, it is not necessary to cycle the slide.

- Staying focused down range, and using the non-firing hand, place the non-full removed magazine in a pocket

NOTE: It is advantageous to keep all partially loaded mags in the same pocket. When time permits, re-stage the most full mags to the front of your pouch and any incomplete mags toward the back of the pouch.

- re-establish perfect grip and the drill is complete

VIDEO 8.A – TAC RELOAD

HTTP://TACTICSANDPREPAREDNESS.COM/3010-8A

DRILL 2:
REPEAT

- Load all three magazines to capacity with three DUMMY rounds each

- Repeat Drill 1 adding drawstroke and dry-firing speed after each round

NOTE: Vary the number of rounds dry-fired before Tac Reloading. Three is not a magic number. The appropriate time is when you can do it and when you believe it will be advantageous.

- Note time

- Repeat the drill perfectly using three magazines of three DUMMY rounds each moving as SLOWLY as is humanly possible (not including the flinging of the cover garment)

NOTE: Firing until empty will necessitate a Combat Reload (instead of Tac Reload).

LOG: Make your entries.

QUESTION OF THE DAY: The next time you are attacked by a violent criminal, would you prefer to have a firearm at hand, or would you not?

DAY 9: IMMEDIATE ACTION, SCANNING

WARNING: Treat all firearms as if they are loaded, Never let the muzzle of a firearm cover anything that you are not willing to destroy, Keep your finger off the trigger and outside of the trigger guard until your sights are aligned on target and you have made the decision to fire, Be certain of your target and aware of the environment around it and behind it!

WARNING: Confirm each round loaded is a non-firing dummy and that there are no live rounds anywhere in the training room.

NOTE: Review your Log entries from yesterday.

DRILL 1:
IMMEDIATE ACTION (DRAWSTROKE FROM OPEN BUTTON DOWN SHIRT)

- Note start time

- Place a nickel sized colored sticker on the wall (your target)

- Load all three magazines to capacity with DUMMY NON-FIRING ROUNDS

- Stand 6' from the target

- Movements should be SLOW

- Load one magazine of Dummy rounds and return to the holster

- Start with both hands relaxed at your sides

- Slowly execute a perfect dry-fire shot

NOTE: This training is for operational situations in which you have a loaded weapon, fire and experience nothing but a "click" or the pistol does not fire.

9. A Tap

NOTE: This is another skill intended to be made an automatic response.

WARNING: A squib round- if the round pops, but does not burn the propellant normally- the projectile may lodge in the barrel; firing another round can cause catastrophe. A squib round sounds distinctly different from a normal round.

9.B Rack

- Responding to the stimulus of "click" when attempting to fire- automatically execute IMMEDIATE ACTION

- (Firmly) **TAP** the bottom of the magazine with the non-firing hand to confirm it is seated

See Image 9.A Tap

- Pivot the non-firing hand to the top of the slide and using the palm and four fingers, rack the slide to the rear (with the weapon still oriented to the target) and reform a perfect grip

NOTE: **RACK** the slide all the way to the rear, continuing your hands movement past the point the slide springs forward.

WARNING: Riding the slide forward with your non- firing hand can induce a malfunction.

See Image 9.B Rack

- **DECIDE** if you need to shoot, if you do, execute a perfect shot

VIDEO – 9.A IA & SCAN (& REHOLSTER)

HTTP://TACTICSANDPREPAREDNESS.COM/3010-9A

LOG: Make your entries.

DRILL 2:
REPEAT

- Conduct the remainder of today's training without eyeglasses on or contact lenses in. This may be uncomfortable but will provide valuable insight into your limitations.

- Load all three magazines to capacity with three DUMMY rounds each

- Repeat Drill 1 deciding that a second shot is not necessary, scanning and re-holster in the reverse sequence of a drawstroke

- Increase speed for each shot

NOTE: After each shot, reconfirm sight picture and that the trigger is staged to threshold, then once the decision is made not to fire again, the finger comes off the trigger, bring the weapon to the Ready or Low Ready (as is appropriate). With the weapon stationary scan as far to your side and behind you as possible then scan to the opposite side and as far behind you as possible.

WARNING: Scanning quickly can overlook threats.

NOTE: Always assume that there is at least one more adversary than you have discovered. They may be behind you. They may appear to be a bystander. They may be camouflaged so that you are not aware of the presence of a person.

- Note time
- Repeat the drill perfectly using three magazines of three DUMMY rounds each moving as SLOWLY as is humanly possible (not including the flinging of the cover garment)

QUESTION OF THE DAY: Why is it critically important for the trigger finger to move entirely independent of the other fingers gripping the pistol?

DAY 10: REMEDIAL ACTION

WARNING: Treat all firearms as if they are loaded, Never let the muzzle of a firearm cover anything that you are not willing to destroy, Keep your finger off the trigger and outside of the trigger guard until your sights are aligned on target and you have made the decision to fire, Be certain of your target and aware of the environment around it and behind it!

WARNING: Confirm each round loaded is a non-firing dummy and that there are no live rounds anywhere in the training room.

NOTE: Review your Log entries from yesterday.

DRILL 1:
REMEDIAL ACTION (DRAWSTROKE FROM OPEN BUTTON DOWN SHIRT)

- Note start time

- Place a nickel sized colored sticker on the wall(your target)

- Load all three magazines to capacity with DUMMY NON-FIRING ROUNDS

- Stand 5' from the target

- Movements should be SLOW

- Load one magazine of Dummy rounds and return to the holster

- Start with both hands relaxed at your sides

- Slowly execute a perfect drawstroke (flinging the cover garment open must be executed quickly to work)

NOTE: We will be setting up a "double feed" type malfunction for training purposes.

- Lock the slide to the rear

- Orient the weapon to the ground (so that gravity works for you)

- Place a DUMMY round in the chamber

- Release the slide- a round will be fed from the magazine into the back of the chambered round

NOTE: You have created a "double feed" for training purposes.

CAUTION: A "double feed" is a malfunction that occasionally occurs.

- Execute Remedial Action- orienting the pistol at eye-level as is done for Loading and lock the slide to the rear with the non-firing hand

- Press the magazine release with the firing-hand thumb and rip the magazine out with the non- firing hand

CAUTION: The magazine may "stick".

- Quickly rack the slide several times to clear the chamber

NOTE: Racking three times is a common rule-of-thumb, however, if it is obvious that the weapon is clear after the first rack, move on to the next step.

- Load a fresh magazine using the Combat Reload technique and confirm sight picture, and trigger pressured to threshold

- Decide if the shot still needs to be taken

- Execute one perfect dry-fire shot

- Slowly Scan for additional threats

- Slowly Re-holster perfectly using reverse drawstroke

DRILL 2:
REPEAT (FOR REMAINDER OF FIRST MAGAZINE)

- Repeat Drill 1 deciding that a second shot is necessary then scan and re-holster in the reverse sequence of a drawstroke

- Increase speed for each shot

- Dry-fire the remainder of the first magazine, setting up "double feeds"

DRILL 3:
EXECUTE IMMEDIATE ACTION AND REMEDIAL ACTION

NOTE: When a pistol trigger is pressured and the weapon "clicks" or does not fire IMMEDIATELY execute Immediate Action ONCE, if that does not correct the problem, IMMEDIATELY execute Remedial Action.

NOTE: It is highly beneficial to seek cover WHILE executing Immediate or Remedial action.

NOTE: If operating with teammates it is beneficial to advise them "Gun down" and "Gun up" so they may provide security and temporarily take responsibility for your sector of fire.

CAUTION: If operating with teammates it is hazardous to move unpredictably (possibly including seeking cover).

NOTE: If regularly operating with the same teammates, it is beneficial to use a brevity code (similar to using "Winchester" when you're out of ammo) instead of announcing "Gun Down" that an adversary might hear.

VIDEO 10.A IA & REMEDIAL ACTION

HTTP://TACTICSANDPREPAREDNESS.COM/3010-10A

- Execute a perfect Drawstroke and Load

- Scan and return to the holster

- Execute a perfect Drawstroke and one dry-fire shot

- When the weapon "clicks" that is your stimulus to immediately execute Immediate Action

- When the weapon "clicks" a second time that is your stimulus to immediately execute Remedial Action

- Decide that another shot is NOT necessary

- Scan and return to the holster

DRILL 4:
REPEAT DRILL 3

- Add speed for each iteration

- Soak hands in a bowl full of ice and water for as long as is safe and practical. This is to simulate the challenges of reduced finger dexterity.

- Repeat iterations of Drill 3 for remaining time

- Note time

- Repeat Drill 3 perfectly using three magazines of three DUMMY rounds each moving as SLOWLY as is humanly possible (not including the flinging of the cover garment)

30–10 PISTOL TRAINING 45

LOG: Make your entries.

QUESTION OF THE DAY: If you prefer to have access to a firearm for self-defense, and given that you might someday depend on the assistance of a neighbor, would you prefer that trusted neighbors have access to firearms?

DAY 11: DRAWSTROKE FROM CONCEALMENT (PULLOVER)

WARNING: Treat all firearms as if they are loaded, Never let the muzzle of a firearm cover anything that you are not willing to destroy, Keep your finger off the trigger and outside of the trigger guard until your sights are aligned on target and you have made the decision to fire, Be certain of your target and aware of the environment around it and behind it!

WARNING: Confirm each round loaded is a non-firing dummy and that there are no live rounds anywhere in the training room.

NOTE: Review your Log entries from yesterday.

DRILL 1:
DRAWSTROKE FROM SWEATSHIRT (OR LOOSE PULLOVER)

11.A Concealed Draw Pullover 1

CAUTION: A cover garment that is too tight will "print" your weapon and advertise that you are armed.

CAUTION: A cover garment that is too short will reveal your weapon.

- Note start time

- Use a working television in your safe training room with a backstop that will stop live rounds

NOTE: We will conduct training based on an external stimulus. Turn on a news network. The anchorperson will be your training target. Your target will be the precise point equidistant between the anchorperson's nipples. When the anchorperson blinks their eyes, consider that the fire command to execute a perfect drawstroke, a perfect dry-fire shot and re-stage the trigger for the option of another perfect dryfire shot. Focus on the tip of the front sight as always.

- Load all three magazines with three DUMMY NON-FIRING ROUNDS each

- Stand 7' from the target

- Movements should be SLOW

- Load one magazine of Dummy rounds

- Start with both hands relaxed at your sides

See Image 11.A Concealed Draw Pullover 1

- Upon making the decision to draw (stimulus), The non-firing hand moves on the most direct route to grasp the pullover directly in front of the holster

- The non-firing hand raises the pullover, the firing hand follows behind moving vertically, hooking the pistol and drawing with standard grip

11.B Concealed Draw Pullover 2

- Both hands meet at center chest to resume the standard drawstroke and presentation of the pistol

- Fire a perfect dry-fire shot, confirm the sight picture and immediately stage the trigger for a possible follow on shot

- Decide that another shot is unecessary, Scan and reholster using reverse drawstroke

- Repeat the process

See Image 11.B Concealed Draw Pullover 2

VIDEO – 11.A PULLOVER DRAW

HTTP://TACTICSANDPREPAREDNESS.COM/3010-11A

DRILL 2:
COMBAT RELOAD (FROM PULLOVER)

- When you dry-fire all DUMMY rounds in the magazine, lock the slide to the rear

- Rotate the pistol to the Load position with the firing hand

- Simultaneously, the non-firing hand moves directly to the concealed magazine pouch, accesses a fresh magazine of DUMMY rounds and moves directly toward the pistol

- The firing-hand thumb releases the empty magazine and the non-firing-hand immediately (firmly) inserts the fresh magazine of DUMMY rounds

- Both hands meet on the pistol, the non-firing thumb sweeps the slide stop, for redundancy, the firing-hand thumb sweeps the slide stop. Both hands stack in a normal grip while rotating the muzzle toward the target, with sights in front of the dominant eye

- The pistol is projected straight toward the target, stopping at the shooter's perfect ready position, with perfect sight picture, and trigger already staged perfectly for a possible follow on dry-fire shot

- With pistol stationary, scan and reholster with perfect reverse drawstroke

DRILL 3:
REPEAT

- Repeat Drill 1 and 2 adding speed after each magazine is dry-fired

- Note time

- Repeat the drill perfectly using three magazines of three DUMMY rounds each moving as SLOWLY as is humanly possible

LOG: Make your entries.

QUESTION OF THE DAY: Why do you want your focus to be on the tip of the front sight before, during and after "breaking" each shot?

DAY 12: DRAWSTROKE FROM CONCEALMENT (DOUBLE ACTION/ POCKET HOLSTERS)

WARNING: Treat all firearms as if they are loaded, Never let the muzzle of a firearm cover anything that you are not willing to destroy, Keep your finger off the trigger and outside of the trigger guard until your sights are aligned on target and you have made the decision to fire, Be certain of your target and aware of the environment around it and behind it!

WARNING: Confirm each round loaded is a non-firing dummy and that there are no live rounds anywhere in the training room.

NOTE: Review your Log entries from yesterday.

DRILL 1:
DRAWSTROKE FROM POCKET HOLSTER

CAUTION: The use of pocket holsters can be hazardous. Do not violate the safety rules.

NOTE: This drill will be demonstrated with a double-action pistol drawn from a high-quality pocket holster with the safety engaged.

NOTE: If you do not carry a pistol holstered in a pocket holster, skip to Drill 2.

- Note start time

- Use a working television in your safe training room with a backstop that will stop live rounds

NOTE: Todays target will be the center of the news anchor's face, the stimulus will be when the camera focus shifts to a new angle.

12.A Concealed Pocket Holster

- Load three magazines to capacity with DUMMY NON-FIRING ROUNDS

- Stand 5' from the target

- Movements should be SLOW

- Load one magazine of Dummy rounds: (the double action pistol has 1 DUMMY round in the chamber), place the weapon on "safe" and or de-cock, so the hammer is down and "safe" is on

- Place the pistol in the Pocket Holster and place the Pocket Holster in the firing-hand pocket

- Start with both hands relaxed at your sides wearing no cover garment

NOTE: The pistol must not be visible.

See Image 12.A Concealed Pocket Holster

- Upon making the decision to draw (stimulus), The non-firing hand moves directly to the center of the chest, simultaneously the firing hand moves directly to form a perfect grip on the pistol

- The firing hand raises the pistol straight out of the holster, rotating the muzzle to the target as soon as it is clear of the pocket

- When the muzzle is oriented to the target, the sights are aligned to the target, and if the environment behind, before and to the sides of the target is clear of bystanders, the firing hand thumb may sweep the safety off

- Both hands meet at center chest, the non- firing hand's thumb may perform a backup sweep of the safety to ensure disengaging it as a perfect grip is formed.

- If the sights are aligned on target and the decision to dry-fire has been made, the trigger finger may pressure the double action trigger to threshold

- The shooter confirms the tip of the front sight is properly positioned and continues to pressure the trigger straight to the rear, breaking the shot

NOTE: We are resetting the pistol to simulate a second shot.

- Use the non-firing hand, charge the pistol and resume a perfect grip

NOTE: If you are using a double action pistol with a visible hammer you will see the hammer staged to the rear now.

NOTE: A double action pistol fires both double and single action. The previous dry-fire shot was double action (heavier pull). With the hammer to the rear, the shot will be single action (lighter pull).

- Resume a perfect grip and return to the Drill

- Fire a perfect dry-fire shot, confirm the sight picture and immediately stage the trigger for a possible follow on shot

- Decide that another shot is unnecessary, Scan, De-cock/reapply "safe" and return to the holster in a perfect un-hurried reverse drawstroke

- Repeat the Drill

VIDEO – 12.A POCKET HOLSTER DRAW

HTTP://TACTICSANDPREPAREDNESS.COM/3010-12A

CAUTION: The use of Thunderwear can be hazardous. Do not violate the safety rules.

NOTE: This drill will be demonstrated with a double-action pistol drawn from a Thunderwear holster with the safety engaged.

NOTE: If you do not carry a pistol holstered in Thunderwear, skip to Day 13.

DRILL 2:
DRAWSTROKE FROM THUNDERWEAR

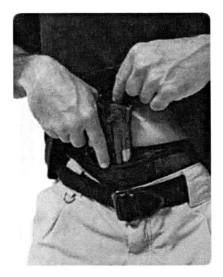

12.B Concealed Thunderwear

- Load three magazines to capacity with DUMMY NON-FIRING ROUNDS

- Stand 5' from the target

- Movements should be SLOW

- Load one magazine of Dummy rounds: (the double action pistol has 1 DUMMY round in the chamber), place the weapon on "safe" and or de-cock, so the hammer is down and "safe" is on

- Place the pistol in the Thunderwear

- Start with both hands relaxed at your sides wearing no additional cover garment (just pants and a shirt)

NOTE: The pistol must not be visible.

See Image 12.B Concealed Thunderwear

- Upon making the decision to draw (stimulus), The non-firing hand lifts the shirt then moves directly to the center of the chest, simultaneously the firing hand moves directly to form a perfect grip on the pistol

- The firing hand raises the pistol straight out of the holster, rotating the muzzle to the target as soon as it is clear of the holster

- When the muzzle is oriented to the target, the sights are aligned to the target, and if the environment behind, before and to the sides of the target is clear of bystanders, the firing hand thumb may sweep the safety off

- Both hands meet at center chest, the non- firing hand's thumb may perform a backup sweep of the safety to ensure disengaging it as a perfect grip is formed.

- If the sights are aligned on target and the decision to dry-fire has been made, the trigger finger may pressure the double action trigger to threshold

- The shooter confirms the tip of the front sight is properly positioned and continues to pressure the trigger straight to the rear, breaking the shot

NOTE: we are resetting the pistol to simulate a second shot.

- Use the non-firing hand, charge the pistol and resume a perfect grip

NOTE: if you are using a double action pistol with a visible hammer you will see the hammer staged to the rear now.

NOTE: a double action pistol fires both double and single action. The previous dry-fire shot was double action (heavier pull). With the hammer to the rear, the shot will be single action (lighter pull).

- Resume a perfect grip and return to the Drill

- Fire a perfect dry-fire shot, confirm the sight picture and immediately stage the trigger for a possible follow on shot

- Decide that another shot is unnecessary, Scan, De-cock/ reapply "safe" and return to the holster in a perfect un-hurried reverse drawstroke

- Repeat the Drill

VIDEO – 12.B THUNDERWEAR DRAW

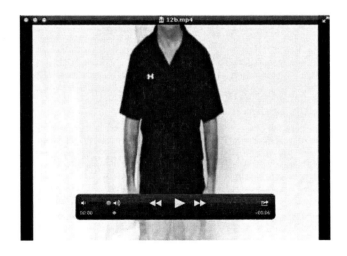

HTTP://TACTICSANDPREPAREDNESS.COM/3010-12B

DRILL 3:
REPEAT

- Repeat Drills 1 and 2 perfectly
- Note time

LOG: Make your entries.

QUESTIONOFTHEDAY: Only a fraction of flights have Federal Air Marshals onboard. How much do you think it would cost to put marshals in every plane, train, bus, school, mall and public event?

DAY 13: DRAWSTROKE FROM CONCEALMENT (SINGLE ACTION/ANKLE HOLSTER)

WARNING: Treat all firearms as if they are loaded, Never let the muzzle of a firearm cover anything that you are not willing to destroy, Keep your finger off the trigger and outside of the trigger guard until your sights are aligned on target and you have made the decision to fire, Be certain of your target and aware of the environment around it and behind it!

WARNING: Confirm each round loaded is a non-firing dummy and that there are no live rounds anywhere in the training room.

NOTE: Review your Log entries from yesterday.

DRILL 1:
DRAWSTROKE FROM ANKLE HOLSTER

CAUTION: The use of ankle holsters can be hazardous. Do not violate the safety rules.

NOTE: This drill will be demonstrated with a single-action pistol drawn from a high-quality ankle holster with the safety engaged.

NOTE: If you do not carry a pistol holstered in an ankle holster, skip to Day 14.

- Note start time

- Use a working television in your safe training room with a backstop that will stop live rounds

13.A Reach to Ankle Holster

NOTE: Todays target will be the point equidistant between the news anchor's nipples, the stimulus will be when the camera focus shifts to a new angle.

- Load three magazines to capacity with DUMMY NON-FIRING ROUNDS

- Stand 7' from the target

- Movements should be SLOW

- Load one magazine of Dummy rounds: (the single action pistol has 1 DUMMY round in the chamber), place the weapon on "safe", so the hammer is to the rear and "safe" is on

- Place the pistol in the Ankle Holster on the inside of the ankle opposite the firing-hand (e.g. inside left ankle for a right handed shooter

- Start with both hands relaxed at your sides wearing long pants

NOTE: The pistol must not be visible.

See Image 13.A Reach to Ankle Holster

- Upon making the decision to draw (stimulus), The non-firing hand moves directly to the lower portion of the non-firing side pants leg

NOTE: The eyes always stay on target.

- The non-firing hand raises the pants leg and the firing-hand immediately draws the pistol straight out of the holster, rotating the muzzle to the target as soon as it is clear of the holster

- When the muzzle is oriented to the target, the sights are aligned to the target, and if the environment behind, before and to the sides of the target is clear of bystanders, the firing hand thumb may sweep the safety off

- Both hands meet at center chest, a perfect grip is formed.

- If the sights are aligned on target and the decision to dry-fire has been made, the trigger finger may pressure the single action trigger to threshold

- The shooter confirms the tip of the front sight is properly positioned, presents the weapon straight out to full presentation and continues to pressure the trigger straight to the rear, breaking the shot

NOTE: We are charging the pistol for a second shot.

- Use the non-firing hand, charge the pistol and resume a perfect grip

NOTE: If you are using a single action pistol with a visible hammer you will see the hammer staged to the rear again.

13.B Present From Ankle Holster

- Resume a perfect grip and return to the Drill

- Fire a perfect dry-fire shot, confirm the sight picture and immediately stage the trigger for a possible follow on shot

- Decide that another shot is unnecessary, Scan

- Charge the pistol and return to the holster in a perfect un-hurried reverse drawstroke placing "safe" on before the muzzle leaves the target

- Repeat the Drill

See Image 13.B Present From Ankle Holster

See Image 13.C Presentation Complete From Ankle Holster

DRILL 2:
REPEAT

- Repeat Drill 1 perfectly

- Note time

13.C Presentation Complete From Ankle Holster

LOG: Make your entries.

QUESTION OF THE DAY: When does a double-action pistol provide a double-action (heavier) trigger pull and when does it provide a single- action (lighter) trigger pull?

DAY 14: THE DRAWSTROKE FROM CONCEALMENT (BUTTON DOWN/STRESS)

WARNING: Treat all firearms as if they are loaded, Never let the muzzle of a firearm cover anything that you are not willing to destroy, Keep your finger off the trigger and outside of the trigger guard until your sights are aligned on target and you have made the decision to fire, Be certain of your target and aware of the environment around it and behind it!

WARNING: Confirm each round loaded is a non-firing dummy and that there are no live rounds anywhere in the training room.

NOTE: Review your Log entries from yesterday.

DRILL 1:
DRAWSTROKE FROM BUTTON DOWN SHIRT (WITH STRESS)

- Begin this session immediately following your aerobic workout (i.e. after your normal run) while your heart rate is still elevated

NOTE: It is best to go immediately into the training drill without delay (no shower or cool down time).

- Note start time

- Use a working television in your safe training room with a backstop that will stop live rounds

NOTE: Today's target will be the center of the news anchor's face, the stimulus will be when the anchor blinks.

- Load three magazines with three DUMMY NON-FIRING ROUNDS each

- Stand 7' from the target

- Movements will be FAST

- Load one magazine of Dummy rounds

- Start with both hands relaxed to the sides

- Upon stimulus, execute a perfect drawstroke, pressing the trigger to threshold as soon as sights are aligned on target and a decision to fire has been made

- Confirm the front sight is positioned as desired while projecting the weapon forward to full presentation

- "Break" the shot as soon as you are ready

- Immediately execute Immediate Action

- Once the sight picture is re-confirmed and trigger slack removed for a possible follow on shot

- Decide another shot is unnecessary, scan, re- holster in a perfect reverse drawstroke

NOTE: Ensure that your focus is always down range NOT down, on your holster.

DRILL 2:
REPEAT

- Load all three magazines with three DUMMY rounds each

- Execute 10 pushups as quickly as possible

- Repeat Drill 1 for speed

- Note time

- Repeat the drill once perfectly using three magazines of three DUMMY rounds each moving as SLOWLY as is humanly possible (not including the flinging of the cover garment)

LOG: Make your entries.

QUESTION OF THE DAY: Given that Assault Rifles have been illegal for decades, and that firearms banned by "Assault Weapons" bans (both past and present) are NOT, by definition, Assault Rifles, do you think this misrepresentation is accidental?

DAY 15: THE DRAWSTROKE FROM CONCEALMENT (BUTTON DOWN/ STRESS/ VIDEO/ SHOT TIMER)

WARNING: Treat all firearms as if they are loaded, Never let the muzzle of a firearm cover anything that you are not willing to destroy, Keep your finger off the trigger and outside of the trigger guard until your sights are aligned on target and you have made the decision to fire, Be certain of your target and aware of the environment around it and behind it!

WARNING: Confirm each round loaded is a non-firing dummy and that there are no live rounds anywhere in the training room.

NOTE: Review your Log entries from yesterday.

DRILL 1:
DRAWSTROKE FROM BUTTON DOWN SHIRT (WITH STRESS).

- Setup video camera to video self training (can be as simple as an iPhone)

- Begin this session immediately following your aerobic workout (ie after your normal run) while your heart rate is still elevated

NOTE: It is best to go immediately into the training drill without delay (no shower or cool down time).

- Note start time

- Use an IPSC cardboard target with nickel-sized color sticker centered on the heart, lungs, spinal cord area in the chest in your safe training room with a backstop that will stop live rounds

NOTE: The sticker is merely a reference point. The torso "A" zone is the target.

- Load three magazines with three DUMMY NON-FIRING ROUNDS each

- Stand 10' from the target

- Ensure the camera is videoing

- Movements will be FAST

- Load one magazine of Dummy rounds

- Start with both hands relaxed to the sides

- Upon stimulus (today the stimulus is the first beep from the shot timer with a 1.1 second par time and random start); execute a perfect drawstroke, breaking the dry-fire shot on the second beep

- Execute Immediate Action

- Scan and re-holster

REVIEW THE VIDEO

- Is your stance perfect? Is your center of gravity rolled forward perfectly? Is your drawstroke perfectly efficient? Did you present the weapon at eye level in front of the dominant eye (or did you duck your head to the weapon)? Did you move the weapon in a perfectly straight line down the line-of-sight to your full presentation position? Were you able to smoothly pressure the trigger straight to the rear to "break" the shot before reaching full extension?

DRILL 2:
REPEAT WITH COMBAT RELOAD

- Load all three magazines with three DUMMY rounds each

- Execute 10 pushups as quickly as possible

- Resume video

- Repeat Drill 1 perfectly (moderate speed, no shot timer)

- Repeat until a Combat Reload is necessary and reload

- Decide another dry-fire shot is not necessary, scan and reholster

REVIEW THE VIDEO

- Is your stance perfect? Is your center of gravity rolled forward perfectly? Is your drawstroke perfectly efficient? Did you present the weapon at eye level in front of the dominant eye (or did you duck your head to the weapon)? Did you move the weapon in a perfectly straight line down the line-of-sight to your full presentation position? Were you able to smoothly pressure the trigger straight to the rear to "break" the shot before reaching full extension?

- Was your Combat Reload perfect? Was the weapon at eye-level (so peripheral vision maintains situational awareness down range)? Did you position the weapon so that gravity pulled the empty magazine out when it was released? Did both hands move together as efficiently as possible? Were you back on target with sights aligned and trigger pressured to threshold as quickly as possible?

DRILL 3:
REPEAT

- Load all three magazines with three DUMMY rounds each

- Execute 10 pushups as quickly as possible

- Repeat Drill 2 perfectly (moderate speed, no shot timer)

- Repeat until a Combat Reload is necessary and reload

- Decide another dry-fire shot is not necessary, scan and reholster

- Note time

LOG: Make your entries.

QUESTION OF THE DAY: Are the two middle fingers providing the tightness for your firing hand grip as tight as you want them, do they immediately go to that level of tension when accessing the pistol, and are they always consistent?

DAY 16: PIVOT DRILLS (WITH BUTTON DOWN SHIRT, CONCEALMENT)

WARNING: Treat all firearms as if they are loaded, Never let the muzzle of a firearm cover anything that you are not willing to destroy, Keep your finger off the trigger and outside of the trigger guard until your sights are aligned on target and you have made the decision to fire, Be certain of your target and aware of the environment around it and behind it!

WARNING: Confirm each round loaded is a non-firing dummy and that there are no live rounds anywhere in the training room.

NOTE: Review your Log entries from yesterday.

DRILL 1:
90 DEGREE PIVOTS (LEFT)

- Begin this session immediately following your aerobic workout (i.e. after your normal run) while your heart rate is still elevated

- Note start time

- Use an IPSC cardboard target with nickel-sized color sticker centered on the heart, lungs, spinal cord area in the chest in your safe training room with a backstop that will stop live rounds

- Load three magazines to capacity with DUMMY NON-FIRING ROUNDS

- Stand 10' from the target

- Movements will be slow

- Load one magazine of Dummy rounds

- Start with both hands relaxed to the sides, facing to your right, (90 degree offset)

- Upon decision to conduct a dry-fire pivot drill, turn your head left to the target

- Step (in a straight line) forward with the right foot to position (in on step) for perfect stance oriented to the target, simultaneously execute a perfect Drawstroke

WARNING: Do not remove the pistol from the holster until facing the target. Drawing the weapon from the holster prior to turning (or too soon, while turning) can result in pointing the weapon at innocent people; DO NOT VIOLATE THE FOUR SAFETY RULES.

- Execute a perfect dry-fire shot

- Execute Immediate Action and dry-fire a perfect shot

- Execute Immediate Action, and decide another shot is unnecessary (after reconfirming the sight picture and pressuring trigger to threshold).

- Release the trigger pressure (finger outside trigger guard), keep the weapon stationary, scan and re-holster

See Image 16.A Pivot Left 1

See Image 16.B Pivot Left 2

See Image 16.C Pivot Left 3

See Image 16.D Pivot Left 4

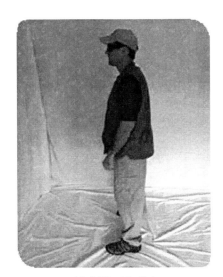

16.A Pivot Left 1

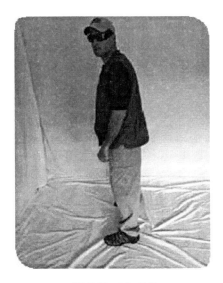

16.B Pivot Left 2

16.C Pivot Left 3

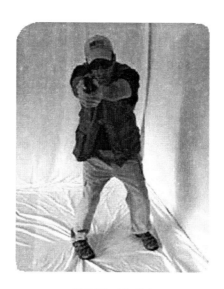

16.D Pivot Left 4

VIDEO – 16.A PIVOT LEFT 90

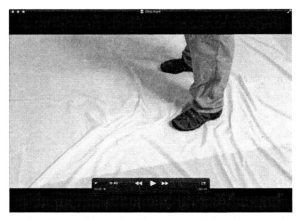

HTTP://TACTICSANDPREPAREDNESS.COM/3010-16A

DRILL 2:
90 DEGREE PIVOTS (RIGHT)

- Stand 10' from the target

- Movements will be slow

- Start with both hands relaxed to the sides, facing to your left, (90 degree offset)

- Upon decision to conduct a dry-fire pivot drill, turn your head right to the target

- Step (in a straight line) forward with the left foot to position (in one step) for perfect stance oriented to the target, simultaneously execute a perfect Drawstroke

WARNING: Do not remove the pistol from the holster until facing the target. Drawing the weapon from the holster prior to turning (or too soon, while turning) can result in pointing the weapon at innocent people; DO NOT VIOLATE THE FOUR SAFETY RULES.

- Execute a perfect dry-fire shot

- Execute Immediate Action and dry-fire a perfect shot

- Execute Immediate Action, and decide another shot is unnecessary (after reconfirming the sight picture and pressuring trigger to threshold).

- Release the trigger pressure (finger outside trigger guard), keep the weapon stationary, scan and re-holster

DRILL 3:
180 DEGREE PIVOTS (LEFT)

- Stand 10' from the target

- Movements will be slow

- Start with both hands relaxed to the sides, facing away from the target

- Upon decision to conduct a dry-fire pivot drill, turn your head to your left, locking eyes on the target

- Step (in a straight line) forward with the right foot to position (in one step) for perfect stance oriented to the target, simultaneously execute a perfect Drawstroke

CAUTION: "Swinging around" rather than stepping straight to the intended foot position is inefficient and clumsy.

WARNING: Do not remove the pistol from the holster until facing the target. Drawing the weapon from the holster prior to turning (or too soon, while turning) can result in pointing the weapon at innocent people; DO NOT VIOLATE THE FOUR SAFETY RULES.

- Execute a perfect dry-fire shot

- Execute Immediate Action and dry-fire a perfect shot

- Execute Immediate Action, and decide another shot is unnecessary (after reconfirming the sight picture and pressuring trigger to threshold)

- Release the trigger pressure (finger outside trigger guard), keep the weapon stationary, scan and re-holster

DRILL 4:
180 DEGREE PIVOTS (RIGHT)

- Stand 10' from the target

- Movements will be slow

- Start with both hands relaxed to the sides, facing away from the target

- Upon decision to conduct a dry-fire pivot drill, turn your head to your right, locking eyes on the target

- Step (in a straight line) forward with the left foot to position (in one step) for perfect stance oriented to the target, simultaneously execute a perfect Drawstroke

CAUTION: Stepping backward rather than forward increases the risk of tripping. Stepping forward is correct.

WARNING: Do not remove the pistol from the holster until facing the target. Drawing the weapon from the holster prior to turning (or too soon, while turning) can result in pointing the weapon at innocent people; DO NOT VIOLATE THE FOUR SAFETY RULES.

- Execute a perfect dry-fire shot

- Execute Immediate Action and dry-fire a perfect shot

- Execute Immediate Action, and decide another shot is unnecessary (after reconfirming the sight picture and pressuring trigger to threshold)

- Release the trigger pressure (finger outside trigger guard), keep the weapon stationary, scan and re-holster

See Image 16.E Pivot Right 180 1

See Image 16.F Pivot Right 180 2

16.E Pivot Right 180 1

16.F Pivot Right 180 2

VIDEO – 16.B PIVOT RIGHT 180

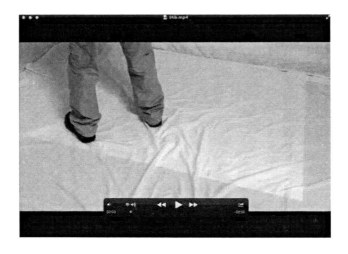

HTTP://TACTICSANDPREPAREDNESS.COM/3010-16B

DRILL 5:
REPEAT

- Execute 10 pushups as quickly as possible

- The colored dot is no longer the target

- The entire IPSC chest "A" zone is the target

- Repeat Drill 1 for speed Repeat Drill 2 for speed Repeat Drill 3 for speed Repeat Drill 4 for speed Repeat all

- Note time

- Repeat Drills 1,2,3,4, once each, perfectly moving as SLOWLY as is humanly possible (not including the flinging of the cover garment); The colored dot is the target

LOG: Make your entries.

QUESTION OF THE DAY: If the flight deck crews of AA flights 11 and 77 and UA flights 93 and 175 had not been prevented from being armed on September 11, 2001, how many planes would have been hijacked?

DAY 17: STRONG HAND ONLY (SHO)/ WEAK HAND ONLY (WHO)

WARNING: Treat all firearms as if they are loaded, Never let the muzzle of a firearm cover anything that you are not willing to destroy, Keep your finger off the trigger and outside of the trigger guard until your sights are aligned on target and you have made the decision to fire, Be certain of your target and aware of the environment around it and behind it!

WARNING: Confirm each round loaded is a non-firing dummy and that there are no live rounds anywhere in the training room.

NOTE: Review your Log entries from yesterday.

DRILL 1:
STRONG HAND ONLY (SHO) DRAW FROM BUTTON DOWN SHIRT (WITH STRESS)

- Begin this session immediately following your aerobic workout (i.e. after your normal run) while your heart rate is still elevated

- Note start time

- Use an IPSC cardboard target with nickel-sized color sticker centered on the heart, lungs, spinal cord area in the chest in your safe training room with a backstop that will stop live rounds

- Load three magazines with three DUMMY NON-FIRING ROUNDS each

17.A SHO

- Stand 7' from the target

- Load one magazine of Dummy rounds

- Start with the firing-hand relaxed to the side, and the non-firing hand clinched in a fist tight to the center of the chest

See Image 17.A SHO

NOTE: We are simulating that the non-firing hand is incapacitated.

- Upon the decision to dry-fire, execute a strong hand only drawstroke; this is the same as a normal drawstroke, without meeting the non- firing hand. The weapon is presented in front of the dominant eye and projected forward

- When sights are aligned on target and the decision to dry-fire is made, the trigger is pressured to threshold

- Sight picture is confirmed and the trigger finger breaks the shot

DRILL 2:
STRONG HAND ONLY (SHO) IMMEDIATE ACTION

17.B SHO Knee Tap

- While standing, use the knee to tap the magazine

  See Image 17.B SHO Knee Tap
- Hook the rear sight on your pocket, press into your leg

- Rack the slide using the strong hand only

WARNING: Performing this step incorrectly could violate the Four Safety Rules.

See Image 17.C SHO Rack

- Aim the weapon and decide that it is not necessary to fire

- Scan, re-holster

17.C SHO Rack

VIDEO – 17.A SHO IA

HTTP://TACTICSANDPREPAREDNESS.COM/3010-17A

DRILL 3:
SHO RELOAD

- Using both hands, remove the magazine, lock the slide to the rear, insert an unloaded magazine

NOTE: Begin with the weapon in the firing hand only, aimed at the target, slide locked to the rear, empty magazine inserted, non-firing hand in a fist held to chest.

- Eject the empty magazine and Squat
- Hold the weapon (oriented muzzle to the deck, magazine well toward the target) with your knees

WARNING: Do not violate the Four Safety Rules.

See Image 17.D SHO Combat Reload weapon/knees

- Using the SHO, access a fresh magazine and insert it
- Acquire a perfect SHO grip and stand
- Release the slide SHO
- Aim and decide to fire a perfect dry-fire shot
- Execute SHO Immediate Action
- Decide it is not necessary to dry-fire
- Scan and re-holster

17.D SHO Combat Reload weapon/knees

VIDEO – 17.B SHO COMBAT RELOAD

HTTP://TACTICSANDPREPAREDNESS.COM/3010-17B

17.E WHO Draw 1

17.F WHO Draw 2

DRILL 4:
WEAK HAND ONLY (WHO) DRAW FROM BUTTON DOWN SHIRT (WITH STRESS)

- Load three magazines with three DUMMY NON-FIRING ROUNDS each

- Stand 7' from the target

- Load one magazine of Dummy rounds

- Start with the weak hand relaxed to the side, and the strong hand clinched in a fist tight to the center of the chest

See Image 17.E WHO Draw 1

See Image 17.F WHO Draw 2

NOTE: We are simulating that the strong hand is incapacitated.

VIDEO – 17.C WHO DRAW

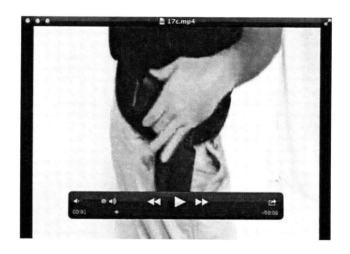

HTTP://TACTICSANDPREPAREDNESS.COM/3010-17C

- Upon the decision to dry-fire, execute a weak hand only drawstroke:

- Withdraw the pistol with the weak hand

- Pivot the pistol, grip forward, and insert it in the holster

- Change grip to perfect weak hand only grip

- WARNING: Do not violate the Four Safety Rules.

- Complete a perfect WHO draw and perfect dry- fire shot

DRILL 5:
WEAK HAND ONLY IMMEDIATE ACTION

- While standing, use the non-firing side knee to tap the magazine
- Hook the rear sight on your pocket, press into your leg
- Rack the slide using the weak hand only
- WARNING: Performing this step incorrectly could violate the Four Safety Rules.
- Aim the weapon and decide that it is not necessary to fire
- scan, re-holster

DRILL 6:
WHO RELOAD

- Using both hands, remove the magazine, lock the slide to the rear, insert an unloaded magazine

NOTE: Begin with the weapon in the weak hand only, aimed at the target, slide locked to the rear, empty magazine inserted, strong hand in a fist held to chest.

- Release the magazine (it may be appropriate to use the trigger finger) and squat
- Hold the weapon (oriented muzzle to the deck, magazine well toward the target) with your knees

WARNING: Do not violate the Four Safety Rules.

- Using the WHO, access a fresh magazine and insert it
- Acquire a perfect WHO grip and stand

- Rack the slide using the pants pocket method if necessary

- Aim and decide to fire a perfect dry-fire shot

- Execute WHO Immediate Action Decide it is not necessary to fire Scan and re-holster

VIDEO – 17.D WHO COMBAT RELOAD

HTTP://TACTICSANDPREPAREDNESS.COM/3010-17D

DRILL 7:
REPEAT

- Execute 10 pushups as quickly as possible

- Repeat Drill 1-6 each time with increasing speed

- Repeat all

- Note time

- Repeat Drills 1-6 once each, perfectly, moving as SLOWLY as is humanly possible

LOG: Make your entries.

QUESTION OF THE DAY: Are you shooting with both eyes completely open for every shot yet?

DAY 18: SHOOTING ON THE MOVE (SOM) FORWARD/ BACKWARD

WARNING: Treat all firearms as if they are loaded, Never let the muzzle of a firearm cover anything that you are not willing to destroy, Keep your finger off the trigger and outside of the trigger guard until your sights are aligned on target and you have made the decision to fire, Be certain of your target and aware of the environment around it and behind it!

WARNING: Confirm each round loaded is a non-firing dummy and that there are no live rounds anywhere in the training room.

NOTE: Review your Log entries from yesterday.

DRILL 1: SOM FORWARD

- Begin this session immediately following your aerobic workout (i.e. after your normal run) while your heart rate is still elevated

NOTE: Shooting on the move is only occasionally beneficial. Most frequently it is advantageous to move swiftly to cover and shoot stationary from cover.

- Note start time
- Use a working television in your safe training room with a backstop that will stop live rounds

NOTE: Today's target will be the center of the news anchor's face, the stimulus will be when the anchor blinks.

- Load three magazines to capacity with DUMMY NON-FIRING ROUNDS

- Stand 15' from the target

- Load one magazine of Dummy rounds

- Start at the Ready and walk toward the target

NOTE: When SOM, the body from the waist up is a perfect firing stance. The legs act as shock absorbers, carrying the weapon along a perfectly straight line. Think of the way a modern tank keeps its' main gun perfectly trained on target even as its' body is maneuvering over obstacles.

NOTE: When SOM, you can only move as quickly as you can shoot accurately.

- Upon stimulus, execute a perfect dry-fire shot

- Hold your finger position on the trigger, reconfirm sight picture and stop walking when at the target

- Execute Immediate Action

VIDEO – 18.A SOM FRONT

HTTP://TACTICSANDPREPAREDNESS.COM/3010-18A

DRILL 2:
SOM BACKWARD

- Starting at the Ready Position at the target, walk backward

NOTE: Use the toes to feel the ground before stepping.

- Break a perfect dry-fire shot when the target blinks

- Confirm the front sight's position and continue walking until at the 15' line

- Stop and execute Immediate Action

NOTE: If you make the decision to use the "shoot on the move" technique backwards, be certain that the benefit outweighs the cost.

WARNING: Walking backwards can result in tripping. Tripping is not an excuse for violating any of the Four Safety Rules.

DRILL 3:
DRAW AND SOM FORWARD

- Begin this session immediately following your aerobic workout (i.e. after your normal run) while your heart rate is still elevated

- Wear an open button down shirt or jacket

- Stand 15' from the target

- Start holstered and walk toward the target

- Upon stimulus, execute a perfect drawstroke and dry-fire shot

- Hold your finger position on the trigger, reconfirm sight picture and stop walking when at the target

- Execute Immediate Action

DRILL 4:
DRAW AND SOM BACKWARD

- Starting holstered at the target, walk backward

- Draw and break a perfect dry-fire shot when the target blinks

- Confirm the front sight's position and continue walking until at the 15' line

- Stop and execute Immediate Action

DRILL 5:
REPEAT

- Load all three magazines to capacity with DUMMY rounds

- Execute 10 pushups as quickly as possible

- Repeat Drill 1 and 2 increasing speed Repeat Drill 3 and 4 increasing speed Note time

- Repeat each drill once perfectly moving at a controlled pace

LOG: Make your entries.

QUESTION OF THE DAY: Do governments that have disarmed their citizens (e.g. The People's Republic of China) treat individuals less callously than governments that know that large portions of their populations retain assault rifles in their homes (e.g. Switzerland)?

DAY 19: SHOOTING ON THE MOVE (TO THE SIDES)

WARNING: Treat all firearms as if they are loaded, Never let the muzzle of a firearm cover anything that you are not willing to destroy, Keep your finger off the trigger and outside of the trigger guard until your sights are aligned on target and you have made the decision to fire, Be certain of your target and aware of the environment around it and behind it!

WARNING: Confirm each round loaded is a non-firing dummy and that there are no live rounds anywhere in the training room.

NOTE: Review your Log entries from yesterday.

DRILL 1:
SOM TO THE NON-FIRING HAND SIDE

- Begin this session immediately following your aerobic workout (i.e. after your normal run) while your heart rate is still elevated

- Note start time

- Use a working television in your safe training room with a backstop that will stop live rounds

- Load three magazines to capacity with DUMMY NON-FIRING ROUNDS

NOTE: Today's target will be the point equidistant between the news anchor's nipples, the stimulus will be when the anchor blinks.

- Load one magazine of Dummy rounds

- Stand 10' from the target, turn 90 degrees to the side so the target is on the non-firing hand side. You are in the middle of the path of travel (½ is behind you, ½ is in front of you). Position yourself at the start of the path (perfectly straight course in front of you) with the target on the non-firing hand side

19.A SOM WH Side

- Start at the Ready (front sight on the target, torso facing the target, legs facing straight forward to the path walk straight forward on the "path"

See Image 19.A SOM WH Side

VIDEO – 19.A SHOOTING ON MOVE WEAK SIDE

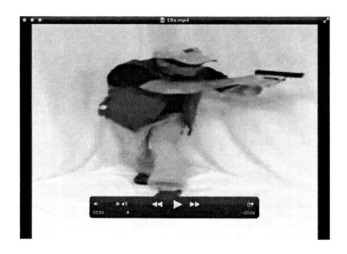

HTTP://TACTICSANDPREPAREDNESS.COM/3010-19A

NOTE: The legs must be capable of walking a perfectly straight line while the torso orients to the target.

- Upon stimulus, execute a perfect dry-fire shot

- Hold your finger position on the trigger, reconfirm sight picture and stop walking when at the end of the "path"

- Execute Immediate Action

DRILL 2:
SOM TO THE FIRING-HAND SIDE

19.B SOM FH side (SHO)

- Stand 10' from the target, turn 90 degrees to the side so the target is on the firing hand side. You are in the middle of the path of travel (½ is behind you, ½ is in front of you). Position yourself at the start of the path (perfectly straight course in front of you) with the target on the firing hand side

- Start at the Ready (front sight on the target, torso facing the target, legs facing straight forward to the path walk straight forward on the "path"

NOTE: The grip will have to transition to a Strong Hand Only grip when it is no longer possible to orient to the target with two hands.

See Image 19.B- SOM FH side (SHO)

VIDEO – 19.B SOM SH SIDE

HTTP://TACTICSANDPREPAREDNESS.COM/3010-19B

- Upon stimulus, execute a perfect dry-fire shot
- Hold your finger position on the trigger, reconfirm sight picture and stop walking when at the end of the "path"
- Execute Immediate Action

DRILL 3:
REPEAT

- Execute 10 pushups as quickly as possible
- Repeat Drill 1 and 2 at increasing speeds
- Note time
- Repeat each drill once perfectly moving at a controlled pace

LOG: Make your entries.

QUESTION OF THE DAY: Are you operating the trigger as efficiently as possible for every shot: moving the trigger finger completely independently of the hand grip tension, smoothly pressuring perfectly straight to the rear only as far as is necessary to "break" the shot and re-setting only as far forward as is necessary to reset the trigger?

DAY 20: SHOOTING FROM COVER

WARNING: Treat all firearms as if they are loaded, Never let the muzzle of a firearm cover anything that you are not willing to destroy, Keep your finger off the trigger and outside of the trigger guard until your sights are aligned on target and you have made the decision to fire, Be certain of your target and aware of the environment around it and behind it!

WARNING: Confirm each round loaded is a non-firing dummy and that there are no live rounds anywhere in the training room.

NOTE: Review your Log entries from yesterday.

DRILL 1:
SHOOTING FROM COVER

- Begin this session immediately following your aerobic workout (i.e. after your normal run) while your heart rate is still elevated
- Note start time

NOTE: Cover protects you from bullets. Concealment protects you from being seen.

- Use an IPSC cardboard target with nickel-sized color sticker centered on the heart, lungs, spinal cord area in the chest in your safe training room with a backstop that will stop live rounds

NOTE: The purpose of using cover is to minimize your exposure to bullets, fragmentation and blast from down range while maximizing your adversaries exposure to your weapon system.

- Load three magazines with three DUMMY NON-FIRING ROUNDS each

- Place the target 10 feet behind a corner

- Load one magazine of Dummy rounds

- Start from behind cover, at the Ready with the weapon oriented to the cover

CAUTION: Unskilled shooters typically "crowd" cover.

NOTE: Remain far enough away from the cover that you can maneuver comfortably with your weapon fully extended and without projecting past cover and giving yourself away unnecessarily.

- Slowly lean out, pie the corner and dry-fire one shot into the IPSC targets chest "A" zone when it is visible

See Image 20.A Effective Use of Cover

See Image 20.B Ineffective Use of Cover

20.A Effective Use of Cover

20.B Ineffective Use of Cover

VIDEO – 20.A PIEING FROM FRONT

HTTP://TACTICSANDPREPAREDNESS.COM/3010-20A

VIDEO – 20.B PIEING FROM BACK

HTTP://TACTICSANDPREPAREDNESS.COM/3010-20B

NOTE: When pieing a corner do not give up area that you have cleared by ducking back behind cover unless that is required for executing Immediate Action, Reloading etc.

CAUTION: If you retreat behind the cover it will be necessary to re-clear (pie) the area you gave up.

- Execute Immediate Action

CAUTION: Bracing against cover may provide an adversary on the other side an opportunity to grab your weapon. If bracing against cover, you are inhibiting your mobility. If you choose to brace against cover for a long shot, ensure that you do not inhibit the function of moving mechanisms.

DRILL 2:
SHOOTING FROM COVER (OPPOSITE SIDE)

- Re-set with the target accessible from the

- opposite side of cover

- Start from behind cover, at the Ready with the weapon oriented to the cover

- Slowly lean out, pie the corner and dry-fire one shot into the IPSC targets chest "A" zone when it is visible

NOTE: Good use of cover may feel like an awkward firing position. Perfect sight picture and perfect trigger operation will deliver perfectly accurate shots.

- Execute Immediate Action

DRILL 3:
REPEAT

- Load all three magazines with three DUMMY rounds each

- Execute 10 pushups as quickly as possible

- Repeat Drill 1 and 2 increasing speed

- Execute Combat Reloads behind cover when necessary

- Note time

- Repeat each drill once perfectly moving at a controlled pace

NOTE: When maneuvering in confined spaces, it may be necessary to temporarily bring the weapon closer (while maintaining muzzle orientation toward the expected target area) to clear an obstacle.

LOG: Make your entries.

QUESTION OF THE DAY: On 13 December, 2012, Min Yingjun stabbed 22 children in one of China's many school attacks. Why do attacks using weapons other than firearms receive so little media interest?

DAY 21: KNEELING/ SQUAT/ MONICA

WARNING: Treat all firearms as if they are loaded, Never let the muzzle of a firearm cover anything that you are not willing to destroy, Keep your finger off the trigger and outside of the trigger guard until your sights are aligned on target and you have made the decision to fire, Be certain of your target and aware of the environment around it and behind it!

WARNING: Confirm each round loaded is a non-firing dummy and that there are no live rounds anywhere in the training room.

NOTE: Review your Log entries from yesterday.

DRILL 1:
SHOOTING FROM A SQUAT

21.A Squat

- Begin this session immediately following your aerobic workout (i.e. after your normal run) while your heart rate is still elevated

- Note start time

- Use a working television in your safe training room with a backstop that will stop live rounds

NOTE: Today's target will be the center of the news anchor's head, the stimulus will be when the camera angle changes.

- Load three magazines with three DUMMY NON-FIRING ROUNDS each

- Stand 7' from the target

- Load one magazine of Dummy rounds

- Start with both hands relaxed to the sides wearing an open concealment shirt

- Upon stimulus, execute a perfect drawstroke, squat, pressing the trigger to threshold as soon as sights are aligned on target and a decision to fire has been made

NOTE: From the waist up the body is identical to a perfect standing position (with forward center of gravity) unless conforming to cover.

- Confirm the front sight is positioned as desired while projecting the weapon forward to full presentation

- "Break" the shot as soon as you are ready

- Immediately execute Immediate Action

- Once the sight picture is re-confirmed and trigger slack removed for a possible follow on shot

- Decide another shot is unnecessary, scan, stand, scan, re-holster in a perfect reverse drawstroke

See Image 21.A Squat

DRILL 2:
SHOOTING MONICA STYLE

- Stand 7' from the target

- Load one magazine of Dummy rounds

- Start with both hands relaxed to the sides wearing an open concealment shirt

- Upon stimulus, execute a perfect drawstroke, drop to both knees, pressing the trigger to threshold as soon as sights are aligned on target and a decision to fire has been made

NOTE: From the waist up the body is identical to a perfect standing position (with forward center of gravity) unless conforming to cover.

- Confirm the front sight is positioned as desired while projecting the weapon forward to full presentation

- "Break" the shot as soon as you are ready

- Immediately execute Immediate Action

- Once the sight picture is re-confirmed and trigger slack removed for a possible follow on shot

- Decide another shot is unnecessary, scan, stand, scan, re-holster in a perfect reverse drawstroke

See Image 21.B Monica

DRILL 3:
KNEELING RIGHT

21.B Monica

- Stand 7' from the target

- Load one magazine of Dummy rounds

- Start with both hands relaxed to the sides wearing an open concealment shirt

- Upon stimulus, execute a perfect drawstroke, drop to the right knee, pressing the trigger to threshold as soon as sights are aligned on target and a decision to fire has been made

NOTE: From the waist up the body is identical to a perfect standing position (forward center of gravity) unless conforming to cover.

21.C Kneel Right Knee Down

- Confirm the front sight is positioned as desired while projecting the weapon forward to full presentation

- "Break" the shot as soon as you are ready

- Immediately execute Immediate Action

- Once the sight picture is re-confirmed and trigger slack removed for a possible follow on shot

- Decide another shot is unnecessary, scan, stand, scan, re-holster in a perfect reverse drawstroke

NOTE: Use cover as aggressively as you do standing (when it is available). The lower body should not be exposed. The knee closest to the edge of cover must be in the air. This allows bracing so that teammates cannot inadvertently bump you from behind cover.

See Image 21.C Kneel Right Knee Down

DRILL 4:
KNEELING LEFT

21.D Kneeling Left Knee Down

- Stand 7' from the target

- Load one magazine of Dummy rounds

- Start with both hands relaxed to the sides wearing an open concealment shirt

- Upon stimulus, execute a perfect drawstroke, drop to the left knee, pressing the trigger to threshold as soon as sights are aligned on target and a decision to fire has been made

NOTE: From the waist up the body is identical to a perfect standing position (forward center of gravity) unless conforming to cover.

- Confirm the front sight is positioned as desired while projecting the weapon forward to full presentation

- "Break" the shot as soon as you are ready

- Immediately execute Immediate Action

- Once the sight picture is re-confirmed and trigger slack removed for a possible follow on shot

- Decide another shot is unnecessary, scan, stand, scan, re-holster in a perfect reverse drawstroke

NOTE: Use cover as aggressively as you do standing (when it is available). The lower body should not be exposed. The knee closest to the edge of cover must be in the air. This allows bracing so that teammates cannot inadvertently bump you from behind cover.

See Image 21.D Kneeling Left Knee Down

DRILL 5:
REPEAT

- Load all three magazines with three DUMMY rounds each

- Execute 10 pushups as quickly as possible

- Repeat Drill 1,2,3 and 4 increasing speed

- Execute Combat Reloads when necessary

- Note time

- Repeat each drill once perfectly moving at a controlled pace

LOG: Make your entries.

QUESTION OF THE DAY: Write down the procedure for Remedial Action. Were the steps correct? Was the sequence correct? Can you do it perfectly without any hesitation?

DAY 22: SEATED SHOOTING

WARNING: Treat all firearms as if they are loaded, Never let the muzzle of a firearm cover anything that you are not willing to destroy, Keep your finger off the trigger and outside of the trigger guard until your sights are aligned on target and you have made the decision to fire, Be certain of your target and aware of the environment around it and behind it!

WARNING: Confirm each round loaded is a non-firing dummy and that there are no live rounds anywhere in the training room.

NOTE: Review your Log entries from yesterday.

DRILL 1:
SHOOTING FROM A SEATED POSITION

- Begin this session immediately following your aerobic workout (i.e. after your normal run) while your heart rate is still elevated

- Note start time

- Use a working television in your safe training room with a backstop that will stop live rounds

NOTE: Today's target will be the point equidistant between the news anchor's nipples, the stimulus will be when the anchor blinks.

- Load three magazines with three DUMMY NON-FIRING ROUNDS each

- Place a chair 10 feet from the target

- Load one magazine of Dummy rounds

- Start seated, with cover garment (open jacket) concealing pistol, and a desk or table in position over your legs, and hands relaxed to the sides

NOTE: The drawstroke will pull the weapon from the holster, extending the distance that it is moved vertically before rotating the muzzle in the direction of the target as much as is necessary to clear the obstruction (desk).

- Upon stimulus, execute a perfect drawstroke and a perfect dry-fire shot

NOTE: While remaining sitting, the upper body rotates center of gravity forward executing a perfect drawstroke.

See Image 22.A Shooting From Seated Draw

See Image 22.B Shooting From Seated Presentation

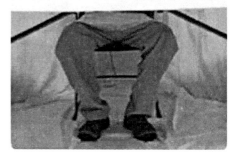

22.A Shooting From Seated Draw

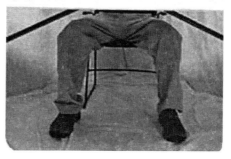

22.B Shooting From Seated Presentation

VIDEO – 22.A SEATED

HTTP://TACTICSANDPREPAREDNESS.COM/3010-22A

- Execute Immediate action

- Decide that another shot is not necessary

- Release the trigger pressure (finger now outside the guard)

- With weapon stationary, scan, and reholster

CAUTION: One of the circumstances when it might be necessary to shoot seated is from a disabled vehicle, or from a passenger seat. Seatbelts and the confinement of a car can fowl drawstrokes. Use seatbelts as is appropriate but always position them so that weapons may be accessed.

NOTE: Shooting from a vehicle, through the windshield will generally cause the rounds path of travel to deviate upward.

NOTE: Shooting into a vehicle, through the windshield will generally cause the rounds path of travel to deviate downward.

NOTE: A functional vehicle is a weapon more deadly than a firearm.

DRILL 2:
REPEAT

- Load all three magazines with three DUMMY rounds each

- Execute 10 pushups as quickly as possible

- Repeat Drill 1 increasing speed on each iteration

- Execute Combat Reloads when necessary

- Note time

- Repeat the drill once perfectly moving at a controlled pace

LOG: Make your entries.

QUESTION OF THE DAY: Do you agree that politicians who advocate disarming citizens should be required to disarm their own personal security details first?

DAY 23: PRONE BRACED/ PRONE/ SUPINE

WARNING: Treat all firearms as if they are loaded, Never let the muzzle of a firearm cover anything that you are not willing to destroy, Keep your finger off the trigger and outside of the trigger guard until your sights are aligned on target and you have made the decision to fire, Be certain of your target and aware of the environment around it and behind it!

WARNING: Confirm each round loaded is a non-firing dummy and that there are no live rounds anywhere in the training room.

NOTE: Review your Log entries from yesterday.

DRILL 1:
SHOOTING PRONE BRACED

- Begin this session immediately following your aerobic workout (i.e. after your normal run) while your heart rate is still elevated

- Wear open button down shirt concealment garment

- Note start time

- Use an IPSC cardboard target folded in half (dividing top and bottom) with nickel-sized color sticker centered on the heart, lungs, spinal cord area in the chest in your safe training room with a backstop that will stop live rounds. Place it on the floor, to simulate distance

NOTE: Prone Braced is useful to minimize the shooters exposure to fire and steady for long distance shots.

- Load three magazines with three DUMMY NON-FIRING ROUNDS each

23.A Prone Braced

- Place the target 7' away and stand

- Load one magazine of Dummy rounds

- Upon initiating, draw the pistol, immediately orienting the muzzle to the target when out of the holster

- Simultaneously place the non-firing hand on the ground to aid in throwing the legs back into a prone position

- As soon as sights are aligned to the target and decision to dry-fire is made, slack should be taken out of the trigger

CAUTION: Do not violate the four safety rules.

NOTE: Bracing the weapon on the deck and creating a cheek-weld with the arm may increase stability for more precise shots.

See Image 23.A Prone Braced

- Focus is, as always, on the front sight tip

- Smoothly pressure the trigger straight to the rear to break the shot as soon as ready

- Execute Immediate Action prone, oriented downrange, rolling partially to side as necessary

- Decide that another shot is not necessary, release trigger pressure (finger outside trigger guard) and scan

- Keeping the muzzle oriented to the target

- come to the knees and resume a two handed grip

- Scan and stand

- Scan and re-holster in a perfect reverse drawstroke

DRILL 2:
SHOOTING PRONE

NOTE: Prone is useful to minimize the shooters exposure to fire, conform to low cover and preserve the ability to traverse the weapon.

- Load three magazines with three DUMMY NON-FIRING ROUNDS each

- Place the folded target 7' away and stand

- Load one magazine of Dummy rounds

- Upon initiating, draw the pistol, immediately orienting the muzzle to the target when out of the holster

- Simultaneously place the non-firing hand on the ground to aid in throwing the legs back into a prone position

23.B Prone

- As soon as sights are aligned to the target and decision to dry-fire is made, slack should be taken out of the trigger

CAUTION: Do not violate the four safety rules.

See Image 23.B Prone

- Focus is, as always, on the front sight tip

- Smoothly pressure the trigger straight to the rear to break the shot as soon as ready

- Execute Immediate Action prone, oriented downrange, rolling partially to side as necessary

- Decide that another shot is not necessary, release trigger pressure (finger outside trigger guard) and scan

- Keeping the muzzle oriented to the target come to the knees and resume a two handed grip

- Scan and stand

- Scan and re-holster in a perfect reverse drawstroke

DRILL 3:
SHOOTING SUPINE

23.C Supine

NOTE: Dry-fire supine is useful to simulate shooting from your back after having been knocked down or making use of unusual cover.

- Place the IPSC target at standard height

- Load three magazines with three DUMMY NON-FIRING ROUNDS each

- Place the target 7' away

- Load one magazine of Dummy rounds

- Upon initiating, draw the pistol, orienting the muzzle to the target

- Simultaneously place the non-firing hand on the ground and get on your back with the weapon oriented to the target

- As soon as sights are aligned to the target and the decision to dry-fire is made, slack should be taken out of the trigger

CAUTION: Do not violate the four safety rules.

NOTE: Getting into the supine position is an administrative act to simulate a shooting position not generally selected on purpose.

See Image 23.C Supine

- Focus is, as always, on the front sight tip

- Smoothly pressure the trigger straight to the rear to break the shot as soon as ready

- Execute Immediate Action supine, oriented downrange

- Decide that another shot is not necessary, release trigger pressure (finger outside trigger guard) and scan

- Keeping the muzzle oriented to the target come forward to a squat and resume a two handed grip

- Scan and stand

- Scan and re-holster in a perfect reverse drawstroke

DRILL 4:
REPEAT

- Load all three magazines with three DUMMY rounds each

- Execute 10 pushups as quickly as possible

- Alternate Drill 1, 2, and 3 increasing speed (not including getting into the supine)

- Execute Combat Reloads prone, or supine when necessary (focused downrange)

- Note time

- Repeat each drill once perfectly moving at a controlled pace

LOG: Make your entries.

QUESTION OF THE DAY: Write down the procedure for a Tactical Reload. Did you get the steps exactly right and in perfect sequence? Can you execute without hesitation?

DAY 24: SHOOTING WITH WHITE LIGHTS

WARNING: Treat all firearms as if they are loaded, Never let the muzzle of a firearm cover anything that you are not willing to destroy, Keep your finger off the trigger and outside of the trigger guard until your sights are aligned on target and you have made the decision to fire, Be certain of your target and aware of the environment around it and behind it!

WARNING: Confirm each round loaded is a non-firing dummy and that there are no live rounds anywhere in the training room.

NOTE: Review your Log entries from yesterday.

DRILL 1:
SHOOTING WITH MOUNTED LIGHT

- Begin this session immediately following your aerobic workout (i.e. after your normal run) while your heart rate is still elevated

- Note start time

- Use an IPSC cardboard target with nickel- sized color sticker centered on the heart, lungs, spinal cord area in the chest in your safe training room with a backstop that will stop live rounds

- Wear an open jacket for concealment

- Load three magazines with three DUMMY NON-FIRING ROUNDS each

- Place the target 10 feet behind a corner

- Darken the training room

- Load one magazine of Dummy rounds

- Start from behind cover, at the Ready with the weapon oriented to the cover

NOTE: If you do not have/use a mounted light, skip to Drill 2.

- Slowly lean out, pie the corner, illuminate the target and dry-fire one shot into the IPSC targets chest "A" zone when it is visible

NOTE: The use of white light should be instantaneous on/illuminate the target/"break" the shot(s)/light off again.

NOTE: Use white light momentarily to develop situational awareness, move swiftly to next point of cover in darkness and briefly strobe the light on again when desired.

24.A Mounted Light Grip

See Image 24.A Mounted Light Grip

- Execute Immediate Action

- Repeat the drill using cover and moving in the opposite direction

- Execute Immediate Action

DRILL 2:
SHOOTING WITH FLASHLIGHT (ONE HANDED)

24.B SHO Flashlight

- Load one magazine of Dummy rounds

- Start from behind cover, at the Ready with the weapon oriented to the cover (Strong Hand Only)

- Slowly lean out, pie the corner, illuminate the target with the light in the non-firing hand and dry-fire one perfect shot into the IPSC targets chest "A" zone when it is visible and release the light button to "off"

See Image 24.B SHO Flashlight

NOTE: Practice minimizing exposure from cover. Also, practice this drill holding the flashlight in different positions to move the light away from your body when desired.

24.C SHO Braced on Flashlight Hand

See Image 24.C SHO Braced on Flashlight Hand

CAUTION: The flashlight is not an aiming device. Do NOT assume the illuminated area is the point of impact.

- Execute Immediate Action

DRILL 3:
SHOOTING WITH FLASHLIGHT (TWO HANDED)

24.D Two Handed Flashlight

- Load one magazine of Dummy rounds

- Start from behind cover, at the Ready with the weapon oriented to the cover (Two Handed)

- Slowly lean out, pie the corner, illuminate the target with the light in the non-firing hand and dry-fire one perfect shot into the IPSC targets chest "A" zone when it is visible and release the light button to "off"

See Image 24.D Two Handed Flashlight

NOTE: Practice minimizing exposure from cover. Also, practice this drill holding the flashlight using multiple two-handed positions.

- Execute Immediate Action

DRILL 4:
REPEAT

- Load all three magazines with three DUMMY rounds each

- Execute 10 pushups as quickly as possible

- Repeat Drill 1, 2, and 3 increasing speed and experimenting with different techniques

- Execute Combat Reloads behind cover when necessary

- Note time

- Repeat each drill once perfectly moving at a controlled pace

- Practice each technique once without eyeglasses or contact lenses.

NOTE: Combat Reloads should be accomplished in darkness. The light (off) can be retained in the hand during the reload, pocketed or hung from a lanyard.

LOG: Make your entries.

QUESTION OF THE DAY: On December 14, 2012, Adam Lanza shot twenty children and six adults at the Sandy Hook Elementary School. If one of those adults had been armed and in possession of the most basic level of fighting skill, how many children might have been saved?

DAY 25: EXTREME CLOSE QUARTERS (FROM CONCEALMENT)

WARNING: Treat all firearms as if they are loaded, Never let the muzzle of a firearm cover anything that you are not willing to destroy, Keep your finger off the trigger and outside of the trigger guard until your sights are aligned on target and you have made the decision to fire, Be certain of your target and aware of the environment around it and behind it!

WARNING: Confirm each round loaded is a non-firing dummy and that there are no live rounds anywhere in the training room.

NOTE: Review your Log entries from yesterday.

DRILL 1:
CLOSE QUARTERS DRAWSTROKE 1 (FROM BUTTON DOWN SHIRT)

25.A CQ Eye Level

- Begin this session immediately following your aerobic workout (i.e. after your normal run) while your heart rate is still elevated

NOTE: All ECQC drawstrokes are derived from the "Full" drawtroke already practiced.

- Note start time
- Use an IPSC cardboard target with nickel-sized color sticker centered on the heart, lungs, spinal cord area in the chest in your safe training room with a backstop that will stop live rounds

NOTE: We are simulating engaging when full extension of the pistol is not viable, but precise accuracy is needed.

- Load three magazines to capacity with DUMMY NON-FIRING ROUNDS
- Stand 4' from the target
- Movements will be FAST
- Load one magazine of Dummy rounds
- Start with both hands relaxed to the sides
- Upon decision to engage the target execute a standard drawstroke, ending with the pistol presented in front of the dominant eye (NOT extending forward), and slack out of the trigger
- Confirm placement of the front sight tip (both eyes open as always), and break a perfect dry- fire shot with smooth pressure
- Execute Immediate Action and execute another perfect dry-fire shot in the same position
- Execute immediate Action and decide another shot is not necessary

- Release trigger pressure, scan and re-holster

See Image 25.A CQ Eye Level

DRILL 2:
CLOSE QUARTERS DRAWSTROKE 2 (FROM BUTTON DOWN SHIRT)

25.B CQ Ready

- Start with both hands relaxed to the sides

- Upon decision to engage the target execute a standard drawstroke, stopping presentation when hands meet in front of the chest (NOT extending forward AND NOT at eye level), and slack out of the trigger

- Sights are aligned with the "A" chest zone (not dot) of the target (even though you can't see them), and break a perfect dry-fire shot with smooth pressure

- Execute Immediate Action and execute another perfect dry-fire shot in the same position

- Execute immediate Action and decide another shot is not necessary

- Release trigger pressure, scan and re-holster

See Image 25.B CQ Ready

DRILL 3:
EXTREME CLOSE QUARTERS DRAWSTROKE (FROM BUTTON DOWN SHIRT)

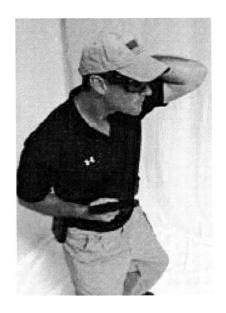

25.C ECQ At Holster

- Start with target at 2' and both hands relaxed to the sides

NOTE: This simulates an extreme close armed attacker, such as an individual unexpectedly pouncing with a knife.

- Upon decision to engage the target, execute a standard drawstroke. As soon as the pistol is clear of the holster and oriented to the target, the pistol should be canted slightly to decrease the chance of the slide action being fouled (in your gear clothing) and the weapon should \ be pinned to your side, remove trigger slack

- Simultaneously duck and redirect non-firing hand to block, creating a shield for the head

- Sights are aligned with the STOMACH/PELVIS of the target

- Pressure the trigger to perfectly simulate the trigger finger movement for three rapid/perfect shots

NOTE: We are not executing Immediate Action until done with the drill.

WARNING: Improper execution of live-fire ECQ Draw can result in shooting yourself.

- Upon completion of the drill, execute Immediate Action

- Scan and re-holster

See Image 25.C ECQ At Holster

DRILL 4:
REPEAT

- Execute 10 pushups as quickly as possible

- Repeat Drill 1, 2, and 3 increasing speed

- Repeat until a Combat Reload is necessary and reload

- Note time

- Conclude with a perfect standard standing stationary drawstroke to dry-fire shot, Immediate Action, scan and re-holster

LOG: Make your entries.

QUESTION OF THE DAY: Write down your description of the perfect and most efficient use of the trigger. When do you remove the slack? When do you pressure through "breaking" point? How far do you move your finger to reset for the next shot? Do you automatically reset (every time) in case there is another shot needed? Do you pressure the trigger smoothly straight to the rear for every shot without "dragging" the pistol frame?

DAY 26: MOVING TARGET (FROM CONCEALMENT)

WARNING: Treat all firearms as if they are loaded, Never let the muzzle of a firearm cover anything that you are not willing to destroy, Keep your finger off the trigger and outside of the trigger guard until your sights are aligned on target and you have made the decision to fire, Be certain of your target and aware of the environment around it and behind it!

WARNING: Confirm each round loaded is a non-firing dummy and that there are no live rounds anywhere in the training room.

NOTE: Review your Log entries from yesterday.

DRILL 1:
MOVING TARGET A

- Begin this session immediately following your
- aerobic workout (i.e. after your normal run) while your heart rate is still elevated
- Note start time
- Use a tennis ball hanging from a string in the center of the training room for a target. The ball should hang to your adam's apple height.

NOTE: The first technique we will practice for engaging a moving target is "tracking"- drawing straight to the target – placing the front sight tip over the intended point of impact- tracking with upper body movement (lower body stationary)- smoothly breaking the dry-fire shot as soon as ready.

- Load three magazines with three DUMMY NON-FIRING ROUNDS each

- Load one magazine of Dummy rounds

- Walk backwards with the tennis ball, until you can hold it (with the string tight) directly above your head

CAUTION: Ensure the entire backstop area is capable of stopping live rounds. Everything in front of you is backstop area.

- Release the ball, execute a perfect drawstroke to the target, pressing the trigger to threshold

- As soon as the target apexes and begins its re turn swing, confirm the front sight tip is positioned as desired and smoothly break a perfect dry-fire shot

- Immediately execute Immediate Action

- Decide another shot is unnecessary, scan, re- holster in a perfect reverse drawstroke

DRILL 2:
MOVING TARGET B

- Use a tennis ball hanging from a string in the center of the training room. The ball should hang to your adam's apple height.

- Load three magazines with three DUMMY NON-FIRING ROUNDS each

- Load one magazine of Dummy rounds

- Walk backwards with the tennis ball, until you can hold it (with the string tight) directly above your head

CAUTION: Ensure the entire backstop area is capable of stopping live rounds. Everything in front of you is backstop area.

- Release the ball, execute a perfect drawstroke to the target

- confirm the front sight tip is positioned as desired and smoothly break a perfect dry-fire shot BEFORE the ball apexes

- Immediately execute Immediate Action

- Decide another shot is unnecessary, scan, re- holster in a perfect reverse drawstroke

DRILL 3:
MOVING TARGET C

- Use a tennis ball hanging from a string in the center of the training room for a target. The ball should hang to your adam's apple height.

NOTE: The second technique we will practice for engaging a moving target is "ambush"- drawing straight to a point you expect the target to pass (and taking out trigger slack). When the leading edge of the moving target moves behind the front sight tip, smoothly/ instantaneously break the dry- fire shot.

- Load three magazines with three DUMMY NON-FIRING ROUNDS each

- Load one magazine of Dummy rounds

- Walk backwards with the tennis ball, hold it as far to your left as you can (with the string tight)

CAUTION: Ensure the entire backstop area is capable of stopping live rounds. Everything in front of you is backstop area.

- Release the ball, execute a perfect drawstroke

- As soon as the target apexes and begins its return swing, confirm the front sight tip is positioned as desired and smoothly break a perfect dry-fire shot

- Execute Immediate Action

- scan, and re-holster in a perfect reverse drawstroke

DRILL 4:
MOVING TARGET D

- Use a tennis ball hanging from a string in the center of the training room. The ball should hang to your adam's apple height.

- Load three magazines with three DUMMY NON-FIRING ROUNDS each

- Load one magazine of Dummy rounds

- Walk backwards with the tennis ball, hold it as far to your right as you can (with the string tight)

CAUTION: Ensure the entire backstop area is capable of stopping live rounds. Everything in front of you is backstop area.

- Release the ball, execute a perfect drawstroke

- confirm the front sight tip is positioned as desired and smoothly break a perfect dry-fire

- Execute Immediate Action

- scan, re-holster in a perfect reverse drawstroke

DRILL 5:
REPEAT

- Load all three magazines with three DUMMY rounds each

- Execute 10 pushups as quickly as possible

- Repeat Drills 1, 2, 3, and 4 for duration of time. Experiment with "tracking" and "ambush". Attempt dry-fire shots after the apex and before

- Execute Combat Reloads when necessary

- Note time

LOG: Make your entries.

QUESTION OF THE DAY: "God made man, but Sam Colt made them equal" – did you know that this quote refers to the fact that Colt's widespread distribution of handguns was the technological innovation that enabled the small and weak to escape the whims of the bigger and stronger?

DAY 27: MULTIPLE TARGETS (FROM CONCEALMENT)

WARNING: Treat all firearms as if they are loaded, Never let the muzzle of a firearm cover anything that you are not willing to destroy, Keep your finger off the trigger and outside of the trigger guard until your sights are aligned on target and you have made the decision to fire, Be certain of your target and aware of the environment around it and behind it!

WARNING: Confirm each round loaded is a non-firing dummy and that there are no live rounds anywhere in the training room.

NOTE: Review your Log entries from yesterday.

DRILL 1:
MULTIPLE TARGETS (FROM OPEN BUTTON DOWN SHIRT)

- Begin this session immediately following your aerobic workout (i.e. after your normal run) while your heart rate is still elevated

- Note start time

- Use an IPSC cardboard target with nickel-sized color sticker centered on the heart, lungs, spinal cord area in the chest in your safe training room with a backstop that will stop live rounds 6' away

- Use an IPSC cardboard target with nickel-sized color sticker centered on the heart, lungs, spinal cord area in the chest in your safe training room with a backstop that will stop live rounds 6' away 90 degrees to the side

- Load three magazines to capacity with DUMMY NON-FIRING ROUNDS

- Movements will be FAST

- Load one magazine of Dummy rounds

- Start with both hands relaxed to the sides

- Upon decision to engage the target, execute a standard drawstroke straight to the front target

- As soon as the first dry-fire shot is broken,

- the eyes leave the front sight tip and transition swiftly to the 2nd target, the body pivots (with feet stationary), the focus returns to the front sight tip

CAUTION: Transitioning targets before the shot breaks throws the shot off target.

- Move the trigger finger as though rapidly dry- firing two perfect shots into the 2nd target

- As soon as the 2nd simulated dry-fire shot is taken on target #2, the eyes swiftly transition back to target #1

- Return focus to the front sight tip on target #1 and simulate dry-firing one more perfect shot into target #1

- Execute Immediate Action and decide another shot is not necessary

- Release trigger pressure, scan and re-holster

NOTE: This drill simulates firing one round into a primary attacker, swiftly firing two rounds into a second attacker and rapidly returning to the 1st to deliver a second shot.

VIDEO – 27.A MULTI TARGETS

HTTP://TACTICSANDPREPAREDNESS.COM/3010-27A

DRILL 2:
MULTI TARGETS (OPPOSITE DIRECTION)

- Face the IPSC cardboard target that was previously target #2

NOTE: Drill 2 is moving in the opposite direction from Drill 1.

- Load three magazines to capacity with DUMMY NON-FIRING ROUNDS

- Movements will be FAST

- Load one magazine of Dummy rounds

- Start with both hands relaxed to the sides

- Upon decision to engage the target, execute a standard drawstroke straight to the front target

- As soon as the first dry-fire shot is broken, the eyes leave the front sight tip and transition swiftly to the 2nd target, the body pivots (with feet stationary), the focus returns to the front sight tip

CAUTION: Transitioning targets before the shot breaks throws the shot off target.

- Move the trigger finger as though rapidly dry- firing two perfect shots into the 2nd target

- As soon as the 2nd simulated dry-fire shot is taken on target #2, the eyes swiftly transition back to target #1

- Return focus to the front sight tip on target #1 and simulate dry-firing one more perfect shot into target #1

- Execute Immediate Action and decide another shot is not necessary

- Release trigger pressure, scan and re-holster

NOTE: This drill simulates firing one round into a primary attacker, swiftly firing two rounds into a second attacker and rapidly returning to the 1st to deliver a second shot.

DRILL 3:
REPEAT

NOTE: We have spent considerable time developing the precise feel for your trigger. From this drill forward, we will "roll over the curb". If you want to drive over a curb, you don't park against it and then power over it from a stand still. Likewise, from here on out when the decision to fire has been made, we will pressure the trigger to shot without pausing at the breaking point. This is for single and multi-shot engagements.

- Execute 10 pushups as quickly as possible

- Repeat Drills 1, and 2 increasing speed each time

- Perform Combat Reloads as necessary

- Note time

IF YOU ARE DRY-FIRING A SINGLE ACTION PISTOL, do not re-apply the safety until the decision is made to re-holster.

IF YOU ARE DRY-FIRING A DOUBLE ACTION PISTOL, this drill simulates one double action shot followed by three single action shots. Ensure de-cocked before reholstering.

LOG: Make your entries.

QUESTION OF THE DAY: Write down a complete description of a perfect standing drawstroke (stationary target) including trigger work. Did you leave anything out?

DAY 28: SIDESTEP

WARNING: Treat all firearms as if they are loaded, Never let the muzzle of a firearm cover anything that you are not willing to destroy, Keep your finger off the trigger and outside of the trigger guard until your sights are aligned on target and you have made the decision to fire, Be certain of your target and aware of the environment around it and behind it!

WARNING: Confirm each round loaded is a non-firing dummy and that there are no live rounds anywhere in the training room.

NOTE: Review your Log entries from yesterday.

DRILL 1:
SIDESTEP (DRY-FIRE FROM CONCEALMENT)

- Begin this session immediately following your aerobic workout (i.e. after your normal run) while your heart rate is still elevated

- Note start time

- Use a working television in your safe training room with a backstop that will stop live rounds

NOTE: Today's target will be the point equidistant between the news anchor's nipples, the stimulus will be when the camera angle changes.

- Load three magazines to capacity with DUMMY NON-FIRING ROUNDS

- Load one magazine of Dummy rounds

- Place a rectangular coffee table in the center of the room facing the TV with a clear path to walk on all sides

- Start holstered standing behind the table, sidestep passed the edge of the table then walk forward passed the edge of the table, side step passed the opposite edge, walk backward passed the table edge and sidestep behind the table passed the opposite edge

- Upon stimulus, execute a perfect draw, dry-fire, execute Immediate Action, scan, re-holster

NOTE: DO NOT stop moving!

VIDEO – 28.A SIDESTEP BOX

HTTP://TACTICSANDPREPAREDNESS.COM/3010-28A

CAUTION: Do not cross legs and create a trip hazard when side-stepping.

DRILL 2:
REPEAT

- Execute 10 pushups as quickly as possible

- Each time the box pattern is completed, alter movement to the opposite direction

- Repeat Drill 1 at increasing speeds

- Execute Combat Reloads when necessary

- Note time

- Repeat Drill 1 once perfectly in each direction moving at a controlled pace

NOTE: The stimulus provokes your training actions, but actions are conducted to completion, so not every stimulus will inspire a new draw.

LOG: Make your entries.

QUESTION OF THE DAY: As a law enforcement officer, do you want your family members to have unfettered access to the most effective firearms possible to defend themselves with?

DAY 29: SHOOT ON THE MOVE (DIAMONDS)

WARNING: Treat all firearms as if they are loaded, Never let the muzzle of a firearm cover anything that you are not willing to destroy, Keep your finger off the trigger and outside of the trigger guard until your sights are aligned on target and you have made the decision to fire, Be certain of your target and aware of the environment around it and behind it!

WARNING: Confirm each round loaded is a non-firing dummy and that there are no live rounds anywhere in the training room.

NOTE: Review your Log entries from yesterday.

DRILL 1:
SOM (DIAMONDS)

- Begin this session immediately following your aerobic workout (i.e. after your normal run) while your heart rate is still elevated

- Wear an open jacket (concealment garment)

- Note start time

- Use a working television in your safe training room with a backstop that will stop live rounds

NOTE: Today's target will be the center of the news anchor's face, the stimulus will be when the anchor blinks.

- Load three magazines with three DUMMY NON-FIRING ROUNDS each

- Load one magazine of Dummy rounds

- Place four drink coasters on the ground in a di amond pattern with 6'legs and a clear path to walk each leg

- Start holstered standing at the f the diamond from the TV

- Walk the diamond continuously facing the TV

- Upon stimulus, execute a perfect draw, dry- fire, execute Immediate Action, dry-fire, Immediate Action

- scan, re-holster

NOTE: DO NOT stop moving!

VIDEO – 29.A SOM DIAMOND

HTTP://TACTICSANDPREPAREDNESS.COM/3010-29A

DRILL 2:
REPEAT

- Conduct the remainder of today's training without eyeglasses on or contact lenses in. This may be uncomfortable but will provide valuable insight into your limitations.

- Execute 10 pushups as quickly as possible

- Each time the diamond is completed, alter movement to the opposite direction

- Repeat Drill 1 at increasing speeds

- Note time

- Repeat Drill 1 once perfectly in each direction moving at a controlled pace

LOG: Make your entries.

QUESTION OF THE DAY: Write down Day 4 "Drawstroke". Is every detail correct? Is every note, warning and caution accurate? Is it possible to gain any more benefit out of 30/10 than you already have?

DAY 30: (FROM CONFIRM STANDARD DRAWSTROKE CONCEALMENT/ STRESS/ VIDEO/ SHOT TIMER)

WARNING: Treat all firearms as if they are loaded, Never let the muzzle of a firearm cover anything that you are not willing to destroy, Keep your finger off the trigger and outside of the trigger guard until your sights are aligned on target and you have made the decision to fire, Be certain of your target and aware of the environment around it and behind it!

WARNING: Confirm each round loaded is a non-firing dummy and that there are no live rounds anywhere in the training room.

NOTE: Review Day 1-5

DRILL 1:
DRAWSTROKE FROM BUTTON DOWN SHIRT (WITH STRESS)

- Setup video camera to video self training (can be as simple as an iPhone)

- Begin this session immediately following your aerobic workout (ie after your normal run) while your heart rate is still elevated

- Note start time

- Use an IPSC cardboard target with nickel- sized color sticker centered on the heart, lungs, spinal cord area in the chest in your safe training room with a backstop that will stop live rounds

NOTE: The sticker is the target.

- Load three magazines with three DUMMY NON-FIRING ROUNDS each

- Stand 10' from the target

- Ensure the camera is videoing

- Movements will be slow (as fast as necessary to clear button down concealment shirt)

- Load one magazine of Dummy rounds

- Start with both hands relaxed to the sides

- Upon decision to dry-fire execute a perfect drawstroke, breaking the dry-fire shot on the sticker

- Execute Immediate Action

- Scan and re-holster

REVIEW THE VIDEO

- Is your stance perfect? Is your center of gravity rolled forward perfectly? Is your drawstroke perfectly efficient? Did you present the weapon at eye level in front of the dominant eye (or did you duck your head to the weapon)? Did you move the weapon in a perfectly straight line down the line-of-sight to your full presentation position? Were you able to smoothly pressure the trigger straight to the rear to "break" the shot before reaching full extension?

DRILL 2:
REPEAT WITH COMBAT RELOAD

- Load all three magazines with three DUMMY rounds each

- Execute 10 pushups as quickly as possible

- Resume video

- Repeat Drill 1 perfectly (use the chest "A" zone as the target, use the shot timer with 1.2 second par time)

- Repeat until a Combat Reload is necessary and reload

- Decide another dry-fire shot is not necessary, scan and re-holster

REVIEW THE VIDEO

- Is your stance perfect? Is your center of gravity rolled forward perfectly? Is your drawstroke perfectly efficient? Did you present the weapon at eye level in front of the dominant eye (or did you duck your head to the weapon)? Did you move the weapon in a perfectly straight line down the line-of-sight to your full presentation position? Were you able to smoothly pressure the trigger straight to the rear to "break" the shot before reaching full extension?

- Was your Combat Reload perfect? Was the weapon at eye-level (so peripheral vision maintains situational awareness down range)? Did you position the weapon so that gravity pulled the empty magazine out when it was released? Did both hands move together as efficiently as possible? Were you back on target with sights aligned and trigger pressured to threshold as quickly as possible?

DRILL 3:
REPEAT

- Load all three magazines with three DUMMY rounds each

- Execute 10 pushups as quickly as possible

- Repeat Drill 1 perfectly (moderate speed, no shot timer)

- Repeat until a Combat Reload is necessary and reload

- Decide another dry-fire shot is not necessary, scan and re-holster

- Note time

LOG: Make your entries.

QUESTION OF THE DAY: Have you joined the NRA yet? http://membership.nrahq.org/

CONGRATULATIONS! You have completed 30 days of training. You have just demonstrated greater self-discipline than most human beings will ever experience. Picture what your life will be like when you apply this same (proven) self-discipline in the areas of finance/money, fitness/ training, health/nutrition, spirituality/ education and so on!

Please allow me to give you my thoughts on some frequently asked questions that we have not yet discussed. How many times should I fire? When an individual's actions and the circumstance requires you to engage them, it is rare that one shot will end the threat. Deliver accurate fire until it is clear that the threat is ended. That may mean when an adversary goes down and is no longer bringing their weapons to bear. That may be an adversary disengaging and fleeing. That may be an adversary dropping weapons and surrendering. That may be when you can safely disengage and break contact. Answer: As many times as it takes; being too quick to pause can get you killed.

Where should I shoot lethal-force adversaries? First things first – never shoot at a person that does not merit lethal force. From a risk-based perspective, shooting an adversary from behind or oblique is most advantageous. Face-to- face engagement is most dangerous. Think of what a side facing target looks like. Think of the dimensions of key target areas. Train for this. Of course, all shots must be legally and morally justified.

On the adversary, the heart/spine/lungs area is likely the best combination of effectiveness and viability to hit even if not instantly incapacitating. If those hits do not end the threat, walk your hits to another target, either up to the spinal/ brain connection or down to the pelvis. Sometimes it is necessary to start at the head. Engage what is available when necessary. This may be toes or hands. Do not mistake concealment for cover.

Shooters often withhold fire when an adversary is still accessible. Would your bullets go through a garbage can?

Do you recommend shooting sports such as IDPA? Yes, but... After attending agency firearms training and doing 30-10, I highly recommend participating in IDPA. You will improve speed and accuracy and you will have a more accurate assessment of your capabilities. You will be exposed to other techniques. No matter how good you are (Tier-1 military included), you will be outshot on occasion.

WARNING: All shooting sports contain elements artificial to real-world gunfighting. Do not build bad tactical habits. These can be lethal.

Always be cautious that an adversary that appears compliant may revert to combative. Always assume there is at least one more adversary than the one(s) you are aware of. They may be camouflaged in the environment. They may appear to be an innocent. They may be behind you or out of your line of site. That is one of the reasons we ALWAYS scan 360 degrees before re-holstering. Also, initiative always beats reaction. A professional will develop an efficient drawstroke, but no drawstroke is faster than already having a gun out.

With solid shooting skills (safety, accuracy and efficiency), vision and focus is the next critical factor determining success. When fighter pilots are trained, they spend hours memorizing scan patterns (the sequence of instruments to scan for each maneuver). This is done to gain advantages in efficiency that can be measured in fractions of seconds. Gunfighting is similar. Individuals have the ability to relax focus and generally see the widest area possible. (Try holding a finger up on each side with arms spread. Relax vision and inch those hands forward to where you can see both at the same time.) This is often a useful (focus) skill for patrolling, regularly switching to detailed focus to scan lanes near-to-far and segments right-to-left (for people trained to read left-to-right) and then switching back to wide focus. Movement, shape, shine or color can cue you for detailed focus on a specific point. Once it's time to make a shot, focus must shift to narrow/ detailed focus such as you might use to read a small alarm clock from across a large room; and that focus will be on the tip of your front sight.

Think through this example. You are on a SWAT team making entry. Without being there I can describe efficient use of your focus. As you approach the breach point you may want relaxed focus, taking a mental snapshot of all. You swiftly traverse the threshold and your vision tightens to detailed focus on your primary area of responsibility. Nothing is there, and as you continue to your point of domination you deliberately open your vision wide again for greater awareness. If there had been a target, your detailed focus would instantaneously go to your desired (precise) point of impact (if you are well trained) and your hands would swiftly maneuver the front sight tip into the desired position (you don't maneuver staring at sights) as your skilled trigger finger pressed off perfect shots. Think this through. How can you master this for your mission(s)?

You now have huge advantages over other shooters. You have acquired tremendous precision in your actions. Just as some of the most skilled samurai are believed to have studied archery for more than a year before firing a single arrow, you have fired more than 1000 perfect dry-fire shots and conditioned smooth/efficient trigger operation, perfected consistent grip and conditioned out flinch impulses, before returning to live-fire. Your skills are perishable. Repeat 30-10 drills as frequently as you wish. I recommend that you conduct dry-fire training before and after EVERY live-fire training session. Take every dry-fire shot precisely the same as you do live. Take every live-shot precisely as you do dry. If you can operate the trigger without disturbing the sights dry, you can do the exact same live as long as you do not add any additional inputs!

CAUTION: There is one element of shooting skill that cannot be replicated dry. Multi- shot trigger reset.

Multi-shot trigger reset: immediately reset the trigger only moving as far forward as is necessary to reset, immediately remove trigger slack and smoothly break each additional shot operating the trigger finger entirely separately from the steady hand grip pressure. Confirm the sight tip position before and after each shot. If transitioning to another target confirm tip, break shot, immediately transition, (eyes to target then sight tip) confirm tip, break shot just as we practiced. I recommend multi-shot trigger reset drills and multi- target drills be key components of each of your live-fire training sessions. Some shooters practice firing multiple shots from one confirmation of the front sight tip for extremely fast close range shooting (at the expense of some accuracy).

It is my strongest recommendation that you immediately attend a two day live-fire course with my friends at: TFTT, VATA, Trident Concepts, or any other high-quality instructor.

You are a warrior. You have responsibilities. Never forget your commitment to protecting the life, liberty and property of your fellow Americans. Shooting is only one skill of many necessary for your operational success and survival.

C. Graham

Among the many misdeeds of the British rule in India, history will look upon the act of depriving a whole nation of arms, as the blackest.

Mahatma Gandhi